TALKS TO TEACHERS

BY WILLIAM JAMES

TALKS
TO TEACHERS
on Psychology: and
to Students on some
of Life's Ideals.

INTRODUCTION By PAUL WOODRING

W · W · NORTON & COMPANY

New York · London

First Published in the Norton Library,
1958

W. W. Norton & Company, Inc. is also the publisher of the works of Erik H. Erikson, Otto Fenichel, Karen Horney, Harry Stack Sullivan, and The Standard Edition of the Complete Psychological Works of Sigmund Freud.

W. W. Norton & Company, Inc., 500 Fifth Avenue, New York, NY 10110
W. W. Norton & Company Ltd, 10 Coptic Street, London WC1A 1PU

ISBN 0-393-00165-2

PRINTED IN THE UNITED STATES OF AMERICA

4 5 6 7 8 9 0

Contents

INTRODUCTION

By Paul Woodring

―――――――――

WHEN William James first delivered these talks to the teachers of Cambridge in 1892, American education was entering the greatest period of educational reform in its history. Already the changes were taking place and James saw both the opportunities and the dangers.

The event was a memorable one. Here was the greatest psychologist of his day, the man who did more than any other to prepare the way for the psychological advances of the century to come, speaking to classroom teachers about how they might use psychological knowledge to improve their effectiveness as teachers. For this there was no real precedent. Until his day psychology had been looked upon as a branch of philosophy and few had considered a knowledge of the subject essential to the teacher. It is doubtful that many of the teachers in his audience had studied psychology in college or normal school or had any background or knowledge of it in preparation for these lectures.

Many another scholar, working on the frontiers of knowledge, would have balked at the idea of trying to make his views understandable to such an audience, but it is part of the greatness of William James that he was able to make profound ideas understandable and accepted responsibility for communicating new discoveries and old to the people who could best use them in their daily occupations. In these lectures, which later were repeated in many parts of the country and eventually found their way into print in 1899, James pointed out how the proper application of psychological findings might lead the way to better instruction in all the schools.

In 1892 James was fifty years old and at the height of his intellectual powers. His fame as a psychologist already was secure. *Principles of Psychology*, published two years earlier, had been hailed as "a work of genius such as is rare in any language and in any country." Even his critics acclaimed him. One who disagreed with some of his views conceded that "His work will live—if only through the charm of its literary expression—when most textbooks lie dusty and forgotten."

And lived it has. James' *Principles* (including a shorter version titled *Briefer Course* and affectionately known to a generation of college students as "The Jimmy") was the most widely used textbook of psychology for many years and is now found on the list of "The Hundred Great Books" used in many colleges and by adult study groups.

In preparing *Talks to Teachers*, James borrowed many paragraphs and longer passages from his larger book on psychology. The "Talks" is a selection of those parts of his psychological writings most important to teachers with the addition of much new material appropriate to the subject of educational psychology. Although he avoided technical terminology he had no need to rewrite for his new audience, for all that he wrote had the clarity that comes of a superb literary style.

No writer before or since his time has quite equalled James' gift for making psychology interesting and understandable. Compared to the vigorous clarity of his prose, the writing of many latter-day psychologists seems involuted and muddy. Their excessive specialization, great attention to detail, and emphasis on the precise statistical treatment of things that matter little, stands in sharp contrast to his breadth of vision and willingness, at times, to indulge in generalization to make an important point. "I am speaking broadly, I know," he said at the conclusion of one of his talks to students, "and omitting to consider certain qualifications in which I myself believe. But one can only make one point in one lecture, and I shall be well content if I have brought my point home to you this evening in even a slight degree."

It is remarkable that he had become a psychologist at all. When William was a young man psychology had not

yet emerged from its parent discipline, philosophy. A few
medical specialists—today we would call them psychia-
trists—were exploring the problems of psychosis and neu-
rosis, but there was no established field of scholarship or
teaching for a young man interested in the broader field
of psychology—the psychology of normal people. James
later recalled that the first lecture he ever heard on psychology was his own.

His early education gives no clear clue to his choice of
a career. His education was informal and haphazard,
which of course does not at all mean that it was ineffec-
tive or inadequate. Until he was nine his education was
entrusted to a series of governesses. From nine to thirteen
he attended three different private schools in the United
States after which the family set forth on one of their
numerous trips to Europe and during the next five years
William attended a variety of schools in Paris, Boulogne,
Geneva and Bonn, with one brief period in a private
school back in the United States.

By the end of this period he spoke French fluently and
German fairly well, he had acquired a cosmopolitan background of culture and had read very widely and critically.

But by far the most important part of his education
took place at home, for growing up in the home of Henry
James, Senior, was indeed an educational experience. The
entire family read widely and loved the give and take
of intellectual discussion whether frivolous or profound.
At the dinner table the father would throw out some
provocative idea and the entire family would seize upon
it eagerly to prove or to refute. William had an opportunity to test his wits against a whole family of what
would now be called "gifted children," not the least
of whom was his brother Henry, later to become the
novelist.

At nineteen William entered Harvard with the intention of specializing in chemistry. Two years later he came
under the influence of the great biologist, Professor Louis
Agassiz, and was persuaded to transfer to the Department
of Comparative Anatomy and Physiology. He now felt

that he must choose a profession and at about this time wrote in a letter that he had four alternatives: "Natural History, Medicine, Printing and Beggary." Of the serious choices his preference was for natural history, but he saw little chance of making a living at it and chose medicine primarily because it offered the promise of an adequate income.

He entered the Harvard Medical School in the fall of 1864, but though he was successful enough in his studies he found the work distasteful. After a year he postponed his studies to join Professor Agassiz on an expedition up the Amazon, only to find that collecting biological specimens was not much to his liking either. He enjoyed the adventure of the trip but decided that he was cut out for a speculative rather than an active life.

He returned to Harvard in 1866 but again his medical studies were interrupted, this time by illness, and he again went to Europe to recuperate. It was during this interval that the nature of his reading and writing gives definite evidence of a growing interest in psychology, but he was still faced with the necessity of earning a living and he returned to Harvard, where he finally received his M.D. in 1869. This was the only degree he ever earned and it seems a strange one for a man who was to make his mark as a psychologist and philosopher. But the real education of William James was not received in universities and did not lead to degrees.

Although he now had the necessary degree, he remained reluctant to enter into the practice of medicine which he looked upon as sheer drudgery. He was saved from the necessity when, after another period of illness and depression, he was offered a position as instructor in physiology by President Eliot of Harvard, who had been his chemistry teacher ten years earlier.

It was a late vocational choice, for he was already 30, but from this moment on there was never any doubt that his career was to be that of a scholar and a teacher. His health and spirits improved; he liked the academic life and quickly became an able and popular teacher.

Physiology, however, was too restricted a field for a man of such broad-ranging curiosity and in 1876 he offered a new course—the first of its kind in America and one of the first in the world—in physiological psychology. This was a turning point in his career, for it was this course that provided the basis for his entry into the new field. Because of its popularity he was offered a contract by Henry Holt to produce a textbook based on his course. The book, which took him eleven years to complete, was the two-volume *Principles of Psychology*, which made him famous.

James chose to teach psychology because he was interested in both physiology and the philosophy of mind and he saw psychology as a bridge between the two. In presenting psychology as a branch of biology he removed it from the area of speculative philosophy and made it an empirical science. His psychological point of view is that called "Functionalism"—the school of psychology that defines mental phenomena as processes or activities rather than as mental content and emphasizes the usefulness of these activities or functions. This is a very broad approach and it paved the way for the more limited and specialized approaches.

Although he established the first psychological laboratory in this country he was not disposed to do much of the experimental work himself; he preferred to explore ideas and to make hypotheses and to leave the testing to others. Were he alive today he would be delighted to discover how many of his hypotheses have stood the experimental test. He anticipated the theory of conditioning, later demonstrated experimentally by Pavlov, and discusses the principle, without using the word, in his chapter on "Native and Acquired Reactions." In his criticism of associationism he anticipates many elements of the Gestalt school. Other schools of psychology, including Behaviorism and Field Theory, borrowed many of their ideas from James. Today, as these various "schools of psychology" give evidence of merging into a single pattern of experimental psychology, the Functional view of William James remains the foundation for the mainstream of twentieth-century psychology.

There is one curious omission in all of James' psychology. Although he was familiar with the work of his younger contemporary, Sigmund Freud—to whom he refers in *Talks to Teachers* only as "A Viennese neurologist of considerable reputation"—he gives no attention whatever to the importance of sex when he discusses drives and motives in Chapter 7.

He had a lifelong interest in such mental phenomena as hypnotism, dissociation, and mental telepathy and was well aware of the difficulty in trying to reduce psychology to a study of observable behavior alone. Long before he could have read Freud he was aware of the existence of an inner life of which the individual is never fully aware, and when he did read some of Freud's earlier papers he was intrigued by the Freudian concept of the subconscious. But he saw no convincing evidence to support Freud's concept of universal symbolism and was very dubious about his interpretation of dreams. He could not possibly accept psychoanalysis as a scientific method and to James it was important that psychology should become an experimental science—a set of hypotheses to be tested empirically.

At the time *Talks to Teachers* was written, James' major contribution to philosophy was yet to be made and, although the line of inquiry that later led to its development is hinted at in places, one finds in this book no direct reference to pragmatism.

James' philosophical approach has dominated a large segment of American thought in the twentieth century. That it remains the subject of vigorous debate probably would not trouble him a great deal; he saw pragmatism as a method only, "a method of settling metaphysical disputes that might otherwise prove interminable." His view of it was too flexible, tentative, and experimental ever to become a new dogma, and it is not necessary for the reader to accept pragmatism to learn much from *Talks to Teachers*. Although consistent with the pragmatic position, his view of psychology and of teaching preceded its development and is not dependent upon it.

The important facts about William James, as the author of the present volume, are, first that he was a brilliant psychologist and second that he was himself a teacher and, according to all accounts, a remarkably able one who took pride in the teacher's role and recognized its importance. In this latter respect he differed from many of our academic scholars today. Today it is a popular pose of scholars in our higher institutions to say that they know nothing about "education" and are not interested in it. Frequently they look upon themselves as historians, scientists, mathematicians, or classicists but rarely as teachers. In the current agonizing reappraisal of our schools, their principal contribution has been to heap scorn and abuse on the lower schools, the teachers in those schools, and the institutions that prepare teachers for them. Only a few have accepted a responsibility for taking positive steps toward the improvement of learning and of teaching.

Many of our "best" colleges, those of high prestige, large endowments, scholarly faculties, and high academic standards, have turned their backs on the lower schools, have refused or failed to prepare teachers for them, leaving the job of teacher education to institutions of far less adequate resources. The faculties of these better colleges, with only a few exceptions, have shown far more interest in preparing engineers, dentists, lawyers, or business men than in preparing teachers.

William James was far too wise to accept such a view. He saw it as a clear duty of a Harvard professor, a scholar, and a psychologist, to devote some of his best efforts to the improvement of teaching and the education of teachers.

Today we are engaged in a nationwide re-examination of our schools; their philosophy, aims, content and methods. It is this fact that makes this new edition of *Talks to Teachers* a publishing venture of prime importance, for to anyone troubled by the problems of the schools today the voice of William James comes like a fresh breeze across the landscape. Here is none of the caution and indecisiveness so common to much of our contemporary writing on education, none of the defensiveness that causes us to devote our energies to fending off attacks when we should be moving ahead. James saw the need for changes in the educational process and knew that the first step must be a critical evaluation of the status quo. But in his talks there are no reckless attacks upon the schools or the teachers of his day; rather there is a sympathetic appreciation of good teachers and good teaching and an awareness of the great difficulties under which teachers perform their task. He saw the possibility of a new and better education based upon a more complete understanding of the nature of the learner and of the learning process and undertook to convey this understanding to his listeners.

It was surely not his intention that the new emphasis on the processes of teaching and of learning should in any way lessen the attention given in formal education to knowledge, intellectual development, discipline and values. Although he looked upon the intellect itself as a process rather than a faculty, and preferred to speak of intellectual activity rather than of "the intellect," he had the highest regard for the development of intellectual powers as an educational aim.

The years between his day and ours have seen vast changes in all our schools. Universal, free, public education, the great dream of our ancestors, has become a reality in all parts of the nation. Education to the age of sixteen or eighteen is available to and required of all children. High schools, which enrolled only 7 or 8% of the age group when James spoke, now enroll 80 or 85% and higher education is available to an ever-increasing number which is approaching a third of the age-group.

The schools have become infinitely more attractive places with many beautiful buildings, greatly improved equipment, and teachers better prepared for their expanding responsibilities. But the greatest changes have

been in the curriculum, the methods of teaching, and
the philosophy of education which underlies these
changes, and regarding these changes there is much debate. Clearly we have the biggest and the most expensive
educational system in the history of the world; we are less
than certain that we have the best.

Today the educational reforms of the first half of the
twentieth century, including those vaguely grouped together under the title of Progressive Education, have
run their full course, and we have entered into a period
of vigorous reassessment. Progressive Education as a reform movement has come to the end of its day with the
expiration in 1955 of the Progressive Education Association. It has left behind it some valuable legacies and
much confusion.

It is chastening to note, in rereading *Talks to Teachers*, that James anticipated both the important improve-
ments and the excesses that have done so much to offset
the advantages of these reforms. He saw, far more clearly
than many of his followers, that any trend, however
sound, can become ridiculous by being carried to its extreme, and had we listened to him more carefully many
of the problems which have developed in the schools
could have been avoided.

Much of the best of what later came to be called Progressive Education may be found in *Talks to Teachers*:
the concern for the child, the importance of interest as
a motive, the understanding that learning is an active
process and must involve something more than passive
listening. But the weakness and confusions of twentieth-
century educational reforms are not to be found in this
book. James had an acute ear for plausible nonsense and,
great psychologist that he was, he was quick to see the
limitations of psychology. He made it clear that teaching
must always be an art rather than a science, saw the
danger of trying to base the curriculum *entirely* on
childish interests, and the fallacies inherent in Rousseau's
notion that all normal tendencies of the child are in-
herently good and to be encouraged.

In avoiding the mistake, since all too common, of trying to make teaching a science, James said, "Psychology is a science—teaching is an art; and sciences never generate arts directly out of themselves. An intermediary inventive mind must make the application, by use of its originality." In many of our programs of teacher education too little attention has been given to the development of that intermediate inventive mind and too much effort has been devoted to the attempt to encourage all teachers to use similar methods and to reduce teaching to a formula. James would have none of this; he saw that individual differences among teachers is no less important than individual differences among students. He wanted no rigid rules or a strait jacket for the teacher. He reminded us that "many diverse kinds of teaching may equally well agree with psychological laws."

Although he saw the thinking process as central in education, James was not at all reluctant to recommend the use of drill for those activities which must become habitual. He urged that, "We must make automatic and habitual, as early as possible, as many useful actions as we can."

Nor was he reluctant to recommend hard work for himself or for children and even in his own day he feared that education was growing too soft. This will surely come as a surprise to today's elder citizens who are prone to recall that much was demanded of children when they were in school. But, even in 1892, James believed that "Soft pedagogics have taken the place of the old steep and rocky path to learning. But from this lukewarm air the bracing oxygen of effort is left out. It is nonsense to suppose that every step in education *can* be interesting."

To those who read the "Talks" in the nineteen-twenties and thirties much that James had to say sounded a little old-fashioned. His concept of mind and of will seemed dated to psychologists, and educators were prone to reject the values he placed on competition and effort, for this was the day of a softer pedagogy which failed to perceive its own softness. But today these things that

James stressed seem much more sensible than they did twenty or thirty years ago. Psychologists are no longer quite so sure, as were the early behaviorists, that the concepts of mind and of will are useless. In education, too, we seem to have come full cycle, and back to a view that accepts the value of a more vigorous approach to education.

Today, after a long period of controversy and reassessment, we stand on the brink of another great forward movement in American education, a movement which may well bring about changes no less dramatic than those of the first half of the century. Its direction cannot yet be fully identified but it does seem clear that the direction of change will not be the same as that of the period which ended with World War II, and that in some respects it will represent a reversal of trends that have been carried to excess. Today we hear from many quarters a demand for sweeping reforms that will place a greater emphasis on quality, values, clear thinking, and hard work. There is less stress on "growth" and more on learning, less on "needs" and more on accomplishment, less on permissiveness and more on that old-fashioned word, "discipline." The result of these new trends is that the views of William James seem a good deal more sound and realistic today than do those of the leaders of what was called "the new education" a generation ago.

James wanted all teachers to understand the child as a behaving organism and to make use, in their teaching, of all available psychological knowledge concerning the process of learning and its relation to interest, attention, habit, and the association of ideas. He was convinced that this knowledge and understanding would enable them to teach all subjects better. He saw the possibility, however, that the emphasis on the process of learning might, in the hands of less able teachers, lead to a confusion of aims and a lowering of standards. He warned us of the danger and we failed to heed his warning. It is because of this failure that a controversy has arisen between those who wish to place the emphasis in the schools on academic content and those who prefer to stress method or process. Had *Talks to Teachers* been read carefully by all teachers, and by the teachers of teachers, over the past half-century, many of our educational difficulties might have been avoided. James saw clearly that an emphasis on the educational process need in no way weaken the proper intellectual emphasis in education. His view of teaching, and of the role of the teacher, offers a possible basis for the reconciliation of the disastrous conflict between academic scholars and professional educators that has long been a disgrace to our higher institutions.

James was a man of the nineteenth century who built a bridge to the twentieth. He broke sharply with what Santayana called "the genteel tradition" but made the break without jettisoning the cultural heritage. His horizons were broad, his interests almost unbounded; his views were those of a scholar, scientist, and learned man who had travelled widely, and thought deeply. He was thoroughly conversant with the greatest thinkers of his day and with those who had gone before. Like all men of original ideas he was an intellectual rebel but he was a thoughtful one who understood well that which he revolted against.

Because it is easy to read, avoids technical language, and is as the author says in his preface, "practical and popular in the extreme," *Talks to Teachers* is usually regarded as one of James' minor works. But for teachers and parents it is, of all his works, the one that deals most directly with their problems, and it contains the mature thoughts of a wise man. As he speaks to us now, across the years that have witnessed the greatest social and educational change in the history of man, we are made better aware of the timelessness of wisdom.

Preface

In 1892 I was asked by the Harvard Corporation to give a few public lectures on psychology to the Cambridge teachers. The talks now printed form the substance of that course, which has since then been delivered at various places to various teacher-audiences. I have found by experience that what my hearers seem least to relish is analytical technicality, and what they most care for is concrete practical application. So I have gradually weeded out the former, and left the latter unreduced; and now, that I have at last written out the lectures, they contain a minimum of what is deemed 'scientific' in psychology, and are practical and popular in the extreme.

Some of my colleagues may possibly shake their heads at this; but in taking my cue from what has seemed to me to be the feeling of the audiences I believe that I am shaping my book so as to satisfy the more genuine public need.

Teachers, of course, will miss the minute divisions, subdivisions, and definitions, the lettered and numbered headings, the variations of type, and all the other mechanical artifices on which they are accustomed to prop their minds. But my main desire has been to make them conceive, and, if possible, reproduce sympathetically in their imagination, the mental life of their pupil as the sort of active unity which he himself feels it to be. *He* doesn't chop himself into distinct processes and compartments; and it would have frustrated this deeper purpose of my book to make it look, when printed, like a Baedeker's handbook of travel or a text-book of arithmetic. So far as books printed like this book force the fluidity of the facts upon the young teacher's attention, so far I am sure they tend to do his intellect a service, even though they may leave unsatisfied a craving (not altogether without its legitimate grounds) for more nomenclature, head-lines, and subdivisions.

Readers acquainted with my larger books on Psychology will meet much familiar phraseology. In the chapters on habit and memory I have even copied several pages verbatim, but I do not know that apology is needed for such plagiarism as this.

The talks to students, which conclude the volume, were written in response to invitations to deliver 'addresses' to students at women's colleges. The first one was to the graduating class of the Boston Normal School of Gymnastics. Properly, it continues the series of talks to teachers. The second and the third address belong together, and continue another line of thought.

I wish I were able to make the second, 'On a Certain Blindness in Human Beings,' more impressive. It is more than the mere piece of sentimentalism which it may seem to some readers. It connects itself with a definite view of the world and of our moral relations to the same. Those who have done me the honor of reading my volume of philosophic essays will recognize that I mean the pluralistic or individualistic philosophy. According to that philosophy, the truth is too great for any one actual mind, even though that mind be dubbed 'the Absolute,' to know the whole of it. The facts and worths of life need many cognizers to take them in. There is no point of view absolutely public and universal. Private and uncommunicable perceptions always remain over, and the worst of it is that those who look for them from the outside never know *where*.

The practical consequence of such a philosophy is the well-known democratic respect for the sacredness of individuality,—is, at any rate, the outward tolerance of whatever is not itself intolerant. These phrases are so familiar that they sound now rather dead in our ears. Once they had a passionate inner meaning. Such a passionate inner meaning they may easily acquire again if the pretension of our nation to inflict its own inner ideals and institutions *vi et armis* upon Orientals should meet with a resistance as obdurate as so far it has been gallant and spirited. Religiously and philosophically, our ancient national doctrine of live and let live may prove to have a far deeper meaning than our people now seem to imagine it to possess.

CAMBRIDGE, MASS., March, 1899.

TALKS TO TEACHERS

CHAPTER 1

Psychology and the Teaching Art

IN THE general activity and uprising of ideal interests which every one with an eye for fact can discern all about us in American life, there is perhaps no more promising feature than the fermentation which for a dozen years or more has been going on among the teachers. In whatever sphere of education their functions may lie, there is to be seen among them a really inspiring amount of searching of the heart about the highest concerns of their profession. The renovation of nations begins always at the top, among the reflective members of the State, and spreads slowly outward and downward. The teachers of this country, one may say, have its future in their hands. The earnestness which they at present show in striving to enlighten and strengthen themselves is an index of the nation's probabilities of advance in all ideal directions. The outward organization of education which we have in our United States is perhaps, on the whole, the best organization that exists in any country. The State school systems give a diversity and flexibility, an opportunity for experiment and keenness of competition, nowhere else to be found on such an important scale. The independence of so many of the colleges and universities; the give and take of students and instructors between them all; their emulation, and their happy organic relations to the lower schools; the traditions of instruction in them, evolved from the older American recitation-method (and so avoiding on the one hand the pure lecture-system prevalent in Germany and Scotland, which considers too little the individual student, and yet not involving the sacrifice of the instructor to the individual student, which the English tutorial system would seem too often to entail),—all these things (to say nothing of that coeducation of the sexes in whose benefits so many of us heartily believe), all these things, I say, are most happy features of our scholastic life, and from them the most sanguine auguries may be drawn.

Having so favorable an organization, all we need is to impregnate it with geniuses, to get superior men and women working more and more abundantly in it and for it and at it, and in a generation or two America may well lead the education of the world. I must say that I look forward with no little confidence to the day when that shall be an accomplished fact.

No one has profited more by the fermentation of which I speak, in pedagogical circles, than we psychologists. The desire of the schoolteachers for a completer professional training, and their aspiration toward the 'professional' spirit in their work, have led them more and more to turn to us for light on fundamental principles. And in these few hours which we are to spend together you look to me, I am sure, for information concerning the mind's operations, which may enable you to labor more easily and effectively in the several schoolrooms over which you preside.

Far be it from me to disclaim for psychology all title to such hopes. Psychology ought certainly to give the teacher radical help. And yet I confess that, acquainted as I am with the height of some of your expectations, I feel a little anxious lest, at the end of these simple talks of mine, not a few of you may experience some disappointment at the net results. In other words, I am not sure that you may not be indulging fancies that are just a shade exaggerated. That would not be altogether astonishing, for we have been having something like a 'boom' in psychology in this country. Laboratories and professorships have been founded, and reviews established. The air has been full of rumors. The editors of educational journals and the arrangers of conventions have had to show themselves enterprising and on a level with the novelties of the day. Some of the professors have not been unwilling to co-operate, and I am not sure even that the publishers have been entirely inert. 'The new psychology' has thus become a term to conjure up portentous ideas withal; and you teachers, docile and receptive and aspiring as many of you are, have been plunged in an atmosphere of vague talk about our science, which to a great extent has been more mystifying than enlightening. Altogether it does seem as if there were a certain fatality of mystification laid upon the teachers of our day. The matter of their profession, compact enough in itself, has to be frothed up for them in journals and institutes, till its outlines often threaten to be lost in a kind of vast uncertainty. Where the disciples are not independent and critical-minded enough (and I think that, if you teachers in the earlier grades have any defect—the slightest touch of a defect in the world—it is that you are a mite too docile), we are pretty sure to miss accuracy and balance and measure in those who get a license to lay down the law to them from above.

As regards this subject of psychology, now, I wish at the very threshold to do what I can to dispel the mystification. So I say at once that in my humble opinion there *is* no 'new psychology' worthy of the name. There is nothing but the old psychology which began in Locke's time, plus a little physiology of the brain and senses and theory of evolution, and a few refinements of introspective detail, for the most part without adaptation to the teacher's use. It is only the fundamental conceptions of psychology which are of real value to the teacher; and they, apart from the aforesaid theory of evolution, are very far from being new. —I trust that you will see better what I mean by this at the end of all these talks.

I say moreover that you make a great, a very great mistake, if you think that psychology, being the science of the mind's laws, is something from which you can deduce definite programmes and schemes and methods of instruction for immediate schoolroom use. Psychology is a science, and teaching is an art; and sciences never generate arts directly out of themselves. An intermediary inventive mind must make the application, by using its originality.

The science of logic never made a man reason rightly, and the science of ethics (if there be such a thing) never made a man behave rightly. The most such sciences can do is to help us to catch ourselves up and check ourselves, if we start to reason or to behave wrongly; and to criticise ourselves more articulately after we have made mistakes. A science only lays down lines within which the rules of the art must fall, laws which the follower of the art must not transgress; but what particular thing he shall positively do within those lines is left exclusively to his own genius. One genius will do his work well and succeed in one way, while another succeeds as well quite differently; yet neither will transgress the lines.

The art of teaching grew up in the schoolroom, out of inventiveness and sympathetic concrete observation. Even where (as in the case of Herbart) the advancer of the art was also a psychologist, the pedagogics and the psychology ran side by side, and the former was not derived in any sense from the latter. The two were congruent, but neither was subordinate. And so everywhere the teaching must *agree* with the psychology, but need not necessarily be the only kind of teaching that would so agree; for many diverse methods of teaching may equally well agree with psychological laws.

To know psychology, therefore, is absolutely no guarantee that we shall be good teachers. To advance to that result, we must have an additional endowment altogether, a happy tact and ingenuity to tell us what definite things to say and do when the pupil is before us. That ingenuity in meeting and pursuing the pupil, that tact for the concrete situation, though they are the alpha and omega of the teacher's art, are things to which psychology cannot help us in the least.

The science of psychology, and whatever science of general pedagogics may be based on it, are in fact much like the science of war. Nothing is simpler or more definite than the principles of either. In war, all you have to do is to work your enemy into a position from which the natural obstacles prevent him from escaping if he tries to; then to fall on him in numbers superior to his own, at a moment when you have led him to think you far away; and so, with a minimum of exposure of your own troops, to hack his force to pieces, and take the remainder prisoners. Just so, in teaching, you must simply work your pupil into such a state of interest in what you are going to teach him that every other object of attention is banished from his mind; then reveal it to him so impressively that he will remember the occasion to his dying day; and finally fill him with devouring curiosity to know what the next steps in connection with the subject are. The principles being so plain, there would be nothing but victories for the masters of the science, either on the battlefield or in the schoolroom, if they did not both have to make their application to an incalculable quantity in the shape of the mind of their opponent. The mind of your own enemy, the pupil, is working away from you as keenly and eagerly as is the mind of the commander on the other side from the scientific general. Just what the respective enemies want and think, and what they know and do not know, are as hard things for the teacher as for the general to find out. Divination and perception, not psychological pedagogics or theoretic strategy, are the only helpers here.

But, if the use of psychological principles thus be negative rather than positive, it does not follow that it may not be a great use, all the same. It certainly narrows the path for experiments and trials. We know in advance, if we are psychologists, that certain methods will be wrong, so our psychology saves us from mistakes. It makes us, moreover, more clear as to what we are about. We gain confidence in respect to any method which we are using as soon as we believe that it has theory as well as practice at its back. Most of all, it fructifies our independence, and it reanimates our interest, to see our subject at two different angles, —to get a stereoscopic view, so to speak, of the youthful organism who is our enemy, and, while handling him with all our concrete tact and divination, to be able, at the same time, to represent to ourselves the curious inner elements of his mental machine. Such a complete knowledge as this of the pupil, at once intuitive and analytic, is surely the knowledge at which every teacher ought to aim.

Fortunately for you teachers, the elements of the mental machine can be clearly apprehended, and their workings easily grasped. And, as the most general elements and workings are just those parts of psychology which the teacher finds most directly useful, it follows that the amount of this science which is necessary to all teachers need not be very great. Those who find themselves loving the subject may go as far as they please, and become possibly none the worse teachers for the fact, even though in some of them one might apprehend a little loss of balance from the tendency observable in all of us to overemphasize certain special parts of a subject when we are studying it intensely and abstractly. But for the great majority of you a general view is enough, provided it be a true one; and such a general view, one may say, might almost be written on the palm of one's hand.

Least of all need you, merely *as teachers*, deem it part of your duty to become contributors to psychological science or to make psychological observations in a methodical or responsible manner. I fear that some of the enthusiasts for child-study have thrown a certain burden on you in this way. By all means let child-study go on,—it is refreshing all our sense of the child's life. There are teachers who take a spontaneous delight in filling syllabuses, inscribing observations, compiling statistics, and computing the per cent. Child-study will certainly enrich their lives. And, if its results, as treated statistically, would seem on the whole to have but trifling value, yet the anecdotes and observations of which it in part consists do certainly acquaint us more intimately with our pupils. Our eyes and ears grow quickened to discern in the child before us processes similar to those we have read of as noted in the children,—processes of which we might otherwise have remained inobservant. But, for Heaven's sake, let the rank and file of teachers be passive readers if they so prefer, and feel free not to contribute to the accumulation. Let not the prosecution of it be preached as an imperative duty or imposed by regulation on those to whom it proves an exterminating bore, or who in any way whatever miss in themselves the appropriate vocation for it. I cannot too strongly agree with my colleague, Professor Münsterberg, when he says that the teacher's attitude toward the child, being concrete and ethical, is positively opposed to the psychological observer's, which is abstract and analytic. Although some of us may conjoin the attitudes successfully, in most of us they must conflict.

The worst thing that can happen to a good teacher is to get a bad conscience about her profession because she feels herself hopeless as a psychologist. Our teachers are overworked already. Every one who adds a jot or tittle of unnecessary weight to their burden is a foe of education. A bad conscience increases the weight of every other burden; yet I know that child-study, and other pieces of psychology as well, have been productive of bad conscience in many a really innocent pedagogic breast. I should indeed be glad if this passing word from me might tend to dispel such a bad conscience, if any of you have it; for it is certainly one of those fruits of more or less systematic mystification of which I have already complained. The best teacher may be the poorest contributor of child-study material, and the best contributor may be the poorest teacher. No fact is more palpable than this.

So much for what seems the most reasonable general attitude of the teacher toward the subject which is to occupy our attention.

CHAPTER 2

The Stream of Consciousness

I SAID a few minutes ago that the most general elements
and workings of the mind are all that the teacher absolutely
needs to be acquainted with for his purposes.

Now the *immediate* fact which psychology, the science
of mind, has to study is also the most general fact. It is the
fact that in each of us, when awake (and often when
asleep), *some kind of consciousness is always going on.*
There is a stream, a succession of states, or waves, or fields
(or of whatever you please to call them), of knowledge,
of feeling, of desire, of deliberation, etc., that constantly
pass and repass, and that constitute our inner life. The existence of this stream is the primal fact, the nature and
origin of it form the essential problem, of our science. So
far as we class the states or fields of consciousness, write
down their several natures, analyze their contents into elements, or trace their habits of succession, we are on the
descriptive or analytic level. So far as we ask where they
come from or why they are just what they are, we are on
the explanatory level.

In these talks with you, I shall entirely neglect the questions that come up on the explanatory level. It must be
frankly confessed that in no fundamental sense do we know
where our successive fields of consciousness come from, or
why they have the precise inner constitution which they
do have. They certainly follow or accompany our brain
states, and of course their special forms are determined by
our past experiences and education. But, if we ask just *how*

the brain conditions them, we have not the remotest ink-
ling of an answer to give; and, if we ask just how the education moulds the brain, we can speak but in the most abstract, general, and conjectural terms. On the other hand,
if we should say that they are due to a spiritual being called
our Soul, which reacts on our brain states by these peculiar
forms of spiritual energy, our words would be familiar
enough, it is true; but I think you will agree that they
would offer little genuine explanatory meaning. The truth
is that we really *do not know* the answers to the problems
on the explanatory level, even though in some directions of
inquiry there may be promising speculations to be found.
For our present purposes I shall therefore dismiss them entirely, and turn to mere description. This state of things
was what I had in mind when, a moment ago, I said there
was no 'new psychology' worthy of the name.

We have thus fields of consciousness,—that is the first
general fact; and the second general fact is that the concrete fields are always complex. They contain sensations
of our bodies and of the objects around us, memories of
past experiences and thoughts of distant things, feelings of
satisfaction and dissatisfaction, desires and aversions, and
other emotional conditions, together with determinations
of the will, in every variety of permutation and combination.

In most of our concrete states of consciousness all these
different classes of ingredients are found simultaneously
present to some degree, though the relative proportion they
bear to one another is very shifting. One state will seem to
be composed of hardly anything but sensations, another
of hardly anything but memories, etc. But around the sensation, if one consider carefully, there will always be some
fringe of thought or will, and around the memory some
margin or penumbra of emotion or sensation.

In most of our fields of consciousness there is a core of
sensation that is very pronounced. You, for example, now,
although you are also thinking and feeling, are getting
through your eyes sensations of my face and figure, and
through your ears sensations of my voice. The sensations

are the *centre or focus*, the thoughts and feelings the *margin*, of your actually present conscious field.

On the other hand, some object of thought, some distant image, may have become the focus of your mental attention even while I am speaking,—your mind, in short, may have wandered from the lecture; and, in that case, the sensations of my face and voice, although not absolutely vanishing from your conscious field, may have taken up there a very faint and marginal place.

Again, to take another sort of variation, some feeling connected with your own body may have passed from a marginal to a focal place, even while I speak.

The expressions 'focal object' and 'marginal object,' which we owe to Mr. Lloyd Morgan, require, I think, no further explanation. The distinction they embody is a very important one, and they are the first technical terms which I shall ask you to remember.

In the successive mutations of our fields of consciousness, the process by which one dissolves into another is often very gradual, and all sorts of inner rearrangements of contents occur. Sometimes the focus remains but little changed, while the margin alters rapidly. Sometimes the focus alters, and the margin stays. Sometimes focus and margin change places. Sometimes, again, abrupt alterations of the whole field occur. There can seldom be a sharp description. All we know is that, for the most part, each field has a sort of practical unity for its possessor, and that from this practical point of view we can class a field with other fields similar to it, by calling it a state of emotion, of perplexity, of sensation, of abstract thought, of volition, and the like.

Vague and hazy as such an account of our stream of consciousness may be, it is at least secure from positive error and free from admixture of conjecture or hypothesis. An influential school of psychology, seeking to avoid haziness of outline, has tried to make things appear more exact and scientific by making the analysis more sharp. The various fields of consciousness, according to this school, result from a definite number of perfectly definite elementary mental states, mechanically associated into a mosaic or chemically combined. According to some thinkers,—Spencer, for example, or Taine,—these resolve themselves at last into little elementary psychic particles or atoms of 'mind-stuff,' out of which all the more immediately known mental states are said to be built up. Locke introduced this theory in a somewhat vague form. Simple 'ideas' of sensation and reflection, as he called them, were for him the bricks of which our mental architecture is built up. If I ever have to refer to this theory again, I shall refer to it as the theory of 'ideas.' But I shall try to steer clear of it altogether. Whether it be true or false, it is at any rate only conjectural; and, for your practical purposes as teachers, the more unpretending conception of the stream of consciousness, with its total waves or fields incessantly changing, will amply suffice.*

---

* In the light of some of the expectations that are abroad concerning the 'new psychology,' it is instructive to read the unusually candid confession of its founder Wundt, after his thirty years of laboratory-experience:

"The service which it [the experimental method] can yield consists essentially in perfecting our inner observation, or rather, as I believe, in making this really possible, in any exact sense. Well, has our experimental self-observation, so understood, already accomplished aught of importance? No general answer to this question can be given, because in the unfinished state of our science, there is, even inside of the experimental lines of inquiry, no universally accepted body of psychologic doctrine. . . .

"In such a discord of opinions (comprehensible enough at a time of uncertain and groping development), the individual inquirer can only tell for what views and insights he himself has to thank the newer methods. And if I were asked in what for me the worth of experimental observation in psychology has consisted, and still consists, I should say that it has given me an entirely new idea of the nature and connection of our inner processes. I learned in the achievements of the sense of sight to apprehend the fact of creative mental synthesis. . . . From my inquiry into time-relations, etc., . . . I attained an insight into the close union of all those psychic functions usually separated by artificial abstractions and names, such as ideation, feeling, will; and I saw the indivisibility and inner homogeneity, in all its phases, of the mental life. The chronometric study of association-processes finally showed me that the notion of distinct mental 'images' [repro-

CHAPTER 3

The Child as a Behaving Organism

I WISH now to continue the description of the peculiarities of the stream of consciousness by asking whether we can in any intelligible way assign its *functions*.

It has two functions that are obvious: it leads to knowledge, and it leads to action.

Can we say which of these functions is the more essential?

An old historic divergence of opinion comes in here. Popular belief has always tended to estimate the worth of a man's mental processes by their effects upon his practical life. But philosophers have usually cherished a different view. "Man's supreme glory," they have said, "is to be a *rational* being, to know absolute and eternal and universal

---

ducirten Vorstellungen] was one of those numerous self-deceptions which are no sooner stamped in a verbal term than they forthwith thrust non-existent fictions into the place of the reality. I learned to understand an 'idea' as a process no less melting and fleeting than an act of feeling or of will, and I comprehended the older doctrine of association of 'ideas' to be no longer tenable. . . . Besides all this, experimental observation yielded much other information about the span of consciousness, the rapidity of certain processes, the exact numerical value of certain psychophysical data, and the like. But I hold all these more special results to be relatively insignificant by-products, and by no means the important thing."—*Philosophische Studien*, x. 121-124. The whole passage should be read. As I interpret it, it amounts to a complete espousal of the vaguer conception of the stream of thought, and a complete renunciation of the whole business, still so industriously carried on in text-books, of chopping up 'the mind' into distinct units of composition or function, numbering these off, and labelling them by technical names.

truth. The uses of his intellect for practical affairs are therefore subordinate matters. 'The theoretic life' is his soul's
genuine concern." Nothing can be more different in its
results for our personal attitude than to take sides with one
or the other of these views, and emphasize the practical or
the theoretical ideal. In the latter case, abstraction from the
emotions and passions and withdrawal from the strife of
human affairs would be not only pardonable, but praise-
worthy; and all that makes for quiet and contemplation
should be regarded as conducive to the highest human perfection. In the former, the man of contemplation would be
treated as only half a human being, passion and practical
resource would become once more glories of our race, a
concrete victory over this earth's outward powers of darkness would appear an equivalent for any amount of passive
spiritual culture, and conduct would remain as the test
of every education worthy of the name.

It is impossible to disguise the fact that in the psychology of our own day the emphasis is transferred from the
mind's purely rational function, where Plato and Aristotle,
and what one may call the whole classic tradition in philosophy had placed it, to the so long neglected practical
side. The theory of evolution is mainly responsible for this.
Man, we now have reason to believe, has been evolved from
infra-human ancestors, in whom pure reason hardly existed,
if at all, and whose mind, so far as it can have had any
function, would appear to have been an organ for adapting
their movements to the impressions received from the environment, so as to escape the better from destruction.
Consciousness would thus seem in the first instance to be
nothing but a sort of super-added biological perfection,—
useless unless it prompted to useful conduct, and inexplica-
ble apart from that consideration.

Deep in our own nature the biological foundations of our
consciousness persist, undisguised and undiminished. Our
sensations are here to attract us or to deter us, our memories to warn or encourage us, our feelings to impel, and our
thoughts to restrain our behavior, so that on the whole we
may prosper and our days be long in the land. Whatever of

transmundane metaphysical insight or of practically inap-
plicable æsthetic perception or ethical sentiment we may
carry in our interiors might at this rate be regarded as only
part of the incidental excess of function that necessarily
accompanies the working of every complex machine.

I shall ask you now—not meaning at all thereby to close
the theoretic question, but merely because it seems to me
the point of view likely to be of greatest practical use to
you as teachers—to adopt with me, in this course of lectures, the biological conception, as thus expressed, and to
lay your own emphasis on the fact that man, whatever else
he may be, is primarily a practical being, whose mind is
given him to aid in adapting him to this world's life.

In the learning of all matters, we have to start with some
one deep aspect of the question, abstracting it as if it were
the only aspect; and then we gradually correct ourselves by
adding those neglected other features which complete the
case. No one believes more strongly than I do that what
our senses know as 'this world' is only one portion of our
mind's total environment and object. Yet, because it is the
primal portion, it is the *sine qua non* of all the rest. If you
grasp the facts about it firmly, you may proceed to higher
regions undisturbed. As our time must be so short together,
I prefer being elementary and fundamental to being complete, so I propose to you to hold fast to the ultra-simple
point of view.

The reasons why I call it so fundamental can be easily
told.

First, human and animal psychology thereby become less
discontinuous. I know that to some of you this will hardly
seem an attractive reason, but there are others whom it will
affect.

Second, mental action is conditioned by brain action,
and runs parallel therewith. But the brain, so far as we understand it, is given us for practical behavior. Every current
that runs into it from skin or eye or ear runs out again into
muscles, glands, or viscera, and helps to adapt the animal
to the environment from which the current came. It therefore generalizes and simplifies our view to treat the brain

life and the mental life as having one fundamental kind of purpose.

Third, those very functions of the mind that do not refer directly to this world's environment, the ethical utopias, æsthetic visions, insights into eternal truth, and fanciful logical combinations, could never be carried on at all by a human individual, unless the mind that produced them in him were also able to produce more practically useful products. The latter are thus the more essential, or at least the more primordial results.

Fourth, the inessential 'unpractical' activities are themselves far more connected with our behavior and our adaptation to the environment than at first sight might appear. No truth, however abstract, is ever perceived, that will not probably at some time influence our earthly action. You must remember that, when I talk of action here, I mean action in the widest sense. I mean speech, I mean writing, I mean yeses and noes, and tendencies 'from' things and tendencies 'toward' things, and emotional determinations; and I mean them in the future as well as in the immediate present. As I talk here, and you listen, it might seem as if no action followed. You might call it a purely theoretic process, with no practical result. But it *must* have a practical result. It cannot take place at all and leave your conduct unaffected. If not to-day, then on some far future day, you will answer some question differently by reason of what you are thinking now. Some of you will be led by my words into new veins of inquiry, into reading special books. These will develop your opinion, whether for or against. That opinion will in turn be expressed, will receive criticism from others in your environment, and will affect your standing in their eyes. We cannot escape our destiny, which is practical; and even our most theoretic faculties contribute to its working out.

These few reasons will perhaps smooth the way for you to acquiescence in my proposal. As teachers, I sincerely think it will be a sufficient conception for you to adopt of the youthful psychological phenomena handed over to your inspection if you consider them from the point of

view of their relation to the future conduct of their possessor. Sufficient at any rate as a first conception and as a
main conception. You should regard your professional task
as if it consisted chiefly and essentially in *training the pupil
to behavior;* taking behavior, not in the narrow sense of his
manners, but in the very widest possible sense, as including
every possible sort of fit reaction on the circumstances into
which he may find himself brought by the vicissitudes of
life.

The reaction may, indeed, often be a negative reaction.
Not to speak, *not* to move, is one of the most important of
our duties, in certain practical emergencies. "Thou shalt refrain, renounce, abstain!" This often requires a great effort
of will power, and, physiologically considered, is just as
positive a nerve function as is motor discharge.

CHAPTER 4

Education and Behavior

IN OUR foregoing talk we were led to frame a very simple
conception of what an education means. In the last analysis it consists in the organizing of *resources* in the human
being, of powers of conduct which shall fit him to his social and physical world. An 'uneducated' person is one who
is nonplussed by all but the most habitual situations. On
the contrary, one who is educated is able practically to ex-
tricate himself, by means of the examples with which his
memory is stored and of the abstract conceptions which he
has acquired, from circumstances in which he never was
placed before. Education, in short, cannot be better de-

scribed than by calling it *the organization of acquired habits of conduct and tendencies to behavior.*

To illustrate. You and I are each and all of us educated, in our several ways; and we show our education at this present moment by different conduct. It would be quite impossible for me, with my mind technically and professionally organized as it is, and with the optical stimulus which your presence affords, to remain sitting here entirely silent and inactive. Something tells me that I am expected to speak, and must speak; something forces me to keep on speaking. My organs of articulation are continuously innervated by outgoing currents, which the currents passing inward at my eyes and through my educated brain have set in motion; and the particular movements which they make have their form and order determined altogether by the training of all my past years of lecturing and reading. Your conduct, on the other hand, might seem at first sight purely receptive and inactive,—leaving out those among you who happen to be taking notes. But the very listening which you are carrying on is itself a determinate kind of conduct. All the muscular tensions of your body are distributed in a peculiar way as you listen. Your head, your eyes, are fixed characteristically. And, when the lecture is over, it will inevitably eventuate in some stroke of behavior, as I said on the previous occasion: you may be guided differently in some special emergency in the schoolroom by words which I now let fall.—So it is with the impressions you will make there on your pupil. You should get into the habit of regarding them all as leading to the acquisition by him of capacities for behavior,—emotional, social, bodily, vocal, technical, or what not. And, this being the case, you ought to feel willing, in a general way, and without hair-splitting or farther ado, to take up for the purposes of these lectures with the biological conception of the mind, as of something given us for practical use. That conception will certainly cover the greater part of your own educational work.

If we reflect upon the various ideals of education that are prevalent in the different countries, we see that what they all aim at is to organize capacities for conduct. This is most immediately obvious in Germany, where the explicitly avowed aim of the higher education is to turn the student into an instrument for advancing scientific discovery. The German universities are proud of the number of young specialists whom they turn out every year,—not necessarily men of any original force of intellect, but men so trained to research that when their professor gives them an historical or philogical thesis to prepare, or a bit of laboratory work to do, with a general indication as to the best method, they can go off by themselves and use apparatus and consult sources in such a way as to grind out in the requisite number of months some little pepper-corn of new truth worthy of being added to the store of extant human information on that subject. Little else is recognized in Germany as a man's title to academic advancement than his ability thus to show himself an efficient instrument of research.

In England, it might seem at first sight as if the higher education of the universities aimed at the production of certain static types of character rather than at the development of what one may call this dynamic scientific efficiency. Professor Jowett, when asked what Oxford could do for its students, is said to have replied, "Oxford can teach an English gentleman how to *be* an English gentleman."

But, if you ask what it means to 'be' an English gentleman, the only reply is in terms of conduct and behavior. An English gentleman is a bundle of specifically qualified reactions, a creature who for all the emergencies of life has his line of behavior distinctly marked out for him in advance. Here, as elsewhere, England expects every man to do his duty.

CHAPTER 5

The Necessity of Reactions

IF ALL this be true, then immediately one general aphorism emerges which ought by logical right to dominate the entire conduct of the teacher in the classroom.

No reception without reaction, no impression without correlative expression,—this is the great maxim which the teacher ought never to forget.

An impression which simply flows in at the pupil's eyes or ears, and in no way modifies his active life, is an impression gone to waste. It is physiologically incomplete. It leaves no fruits behind it in the way of capacity acquired. Even as mere impression, it fails to produce its proper effect upon the memory; for, to remain fully among the acquisitions of this latter faculty, it must be wrought into the whole cycle of our operations. Its *motor consequences* are what clinch it. Some effect due to it in the way of an activity must return to the mind in the form of the *sensation of having acted,* and connect itself with the impression. The most durable impressions are those on account of which we speak or act, or else are inwardly convulsed.

The older pedagogic method of learning things by rote, and reciting them parrot-like in the schoolroom, rested on the truth that a thing merely read or heard, and never verbally reproduced, contracts the weakest possible adhesion in the mind. Verbal recitation or reproduction is thus a highly important kind of reactive behavior on our impressions; and it is to be feared that, in the reaction against the old parrot-recitations as the beginning and end of instruction, the extreme value of verbal recitation as an element of complete training may nowadays be too much forgotten.

When we turn to modern pedagogics, we see how enormously the field of reactive conduct has been extended by the introduction of all those methods of concrete object teaching which are the glory of our contemporary schools. Verbal reactions, useful as they are, are insufficient. The pupil's words may be right, but the conceptions corresponding to them are often direfully wrong. In a modern school, therefore, they form only a small part of what the pupil is required to do. He must keep notebooks, make drawings, plans, and maps, take measurements, enter the laboratory and perform experiments, consult authorities, and write essays. He must do in his fashion what is often laughed at by outsiders when it appears in prospectuses under the title of 'original work,' but what is really the only possible training for the doing of original work thereafter. The most colossal improvement which recent years have seen in secondary education lies in the introduction of the manual training schools; not because they will give us a people more handy and practical for domestic life and better skilled in trades, but because they will give us citizens with an entirely different intellectual fibre. Laboratory work and shop work engender a habit of observation, a knowledge of the difference between accuracy and vagueness, and an insight into nature's complexity and into the inadequacy of all abstract verbal accounts of real phenomena, which once wrought into the mind, remain there as lifelong possessions. They confer precision; because, if you are *doing* a thing, you must do it definitely right or definitely wrong. They give honesty; for, when you express yourself by making things, and not by using words, it becomes impossible to dissimulate your vagueness or ignorance by ambiguity. They beget a habit of self-reliance; they keep the interest and attention always cheerfully engaged, and reduce the teacher's disciplinary functions to a minimum.

Of the various systems of manual training, so far as woodwork is concerned, the Swedish Sloyd system, if I may have an opinion on such matters, seems to me by far the best, psychologically considered. Manual training methods, fortunately, are being slowly but surely introduced into all our large cities. But there is still an immense distance to traverse before they shall have gained the extension which they are destined ultimately to possess.

No impression without expression, then,—that is the first pedagogic fruit of our evolutionary conception of the mind as something instrumental to adaptive behavior. But a word may be said in continuation. The expression itself comes back to us, as I intimated a moment ago, in the form of a still farther impression,—the impression, namely, of what we have done. We thus receive sensible news of our behavior and its results. We hear the words we have spoken, feel our own blow as we give it, or read in the by-stander's eyes the success or failure of our conduct. Now this return wave of impression pertains to the completeness of the whole experience, and a word about its importance in the schoolroom may not be out of place.

It would seem only natural to say that, since after acting we normally get some return impression of result, it must be well to let the pupil get such a return impression in every possible case. Nevertheless, in schools where examination marks and 'standing' and other returns of result are concealed, the pupil is frustrated of this natural termination of the cycle of his activities, and often suffers from the sense of incompleteness and uncertainty; and there are persons who defend this system as encouraging the pupil to work for the work's sake, and not for extraneous reward. Of course, here as elsewhere, concrete experience must prevail over psychological deduction. But, so far as our psychological deduction goes, it would suggest that the pupil's eagerness to know how well he does is in the line of his normal completeness of function, and should never be balked except for very definite reasons indeed.

Acquaint them, therefore, with their marks and standing and prospects, unless in the individual case you have some special practical reason for not so doing.

CHAPTER 6

Native Reactions and Acquired Reactions

WE ARE by this time fully launched upon the biological conception. Man is an organism for reacting on impressions: his mind is there to help determine his reactions, and the purpose of his education is to make them numerous and perfect. *Our education means, in short, little more than a mass of possibilities of reaction, acquired at home, at school, or in the training of affairs. The teacher's task is that of supervising the acquiring process.*

This being the case, I will immediately state a principle which underlies the whole process of acquisition and governs the entire activity of the teacher. It is this:—

Every acquired reaction is, as a rule, either a complication grafted on a native reaction, or a substitute for a native reaction, which the same object originally tended to provoke.

The teacher's art consists in bringing about the substitution or complication, and success in the art presupposes a sympathetic acquaintance with the reactive tendencies natively there.

Without an equipment of native reactions on the child's part, the teacher would have no hold whatever upon the child's attention or conduct. You may take a horse to the water, but you cannot make him drink; and so you may take a child to the schoolroom, but you cannot make him learn the new things you wish to impart, except by soliciting him in the first instance by something which natively makes him react. He must take the first step himself. He must *do* something before you can get your purchase on him. That something may be something good or something bad. A bad reaction is better than no reaction at all; for, if bad, you can couple it with consequences which awake him to its badness. But imagine a child so lifeless as to react in *no* way to the teacher's first appeals, and how can you possibly take the first step in his education?

To make this abstract conception more concrete, assume the case of a young child's training in good manners. The child has a native tendency to snatch with his hands at anything that attracts his curiosity; also to draw back his hands when slapped, to cry under these latter conditions, to smile when gently spoken to, and to imitate one's gestures.

Suppose now you appear before the child with a new toy intended as a present for him. No sooner does he see the toy than he seeks to snatch it. You slap the hand; it is withdrawn, and the child cries. You then hold up the toy, smiling and saying, "Beg for it nicely,—so!" The child stops crying, imitates you, receives the toy, and crows with pleasure; and that little cycle of training is complete. You have substituted the new reaction of 'begging' for the native reaction of snatching, when that kind of impression comes.

Now, if the child had no memory, the process would not be educative. No matter how often you came in with a toy, the same series of reactions would fatally occur, each called forth by its own impression: see, snatch; slap, cry; hear, ask; receive, smile. But, with memory there, the child, at the very instant of snatching, recalls the rest of the earlier experience, thinks of the slap and the frustration, recollects the begging and the reward, inhibits the snatching impulse, substitutes the 'nice' reaction for it, and gets the toy immediately, by eliminating all the intermediary steps. If a child's first snatching impulse be excessive or his memory poor, many repetitions of the discipline may be needed before the acquired reaction comes to be an ingrained habit; but in an eminently educable child a single experience will suffice.

One can easily represent the whole process by a brain-diagram. Such a diagram can be little more than a symbolic translation of the immediate experience into spatial terms; yet it may be useful, so I subjoin it.

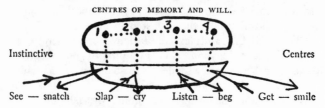

Figure 1. The brain-processes before education.

Figure 1 shows the paths of the four successive reflexes executed by the lower or instinctive centres. The dotted lines that lead from them to the higher centres and connect the latter together, represent the processes of memory and association which the reactions impress upon the higher centres as they take place.

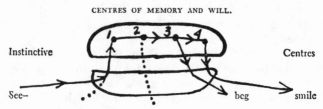

Figure 2. The brain-process after education.

In Figure 2 we have the final result. The impression *see* awakens the chain of memories, and the only reactions that take place are the *beg* and *smile*. The thought of the *slap,* connected with the activity of Centre 2, inhibits the *snatch,* and makes it abortive, so it is represented only by a dotted line of discharge not reaching the terminus. Ditto of the *cry* reaction. These are, as it were, short-circuited by the current sweeping through the higher centres from *see* to *smile*. *Beg* and *smile*, thus substituted for the original reaction *snatch*, become at last the immediate responses when the child sees a snatchable object in some one's hands.

The first thing, then, for the teacher to understand is the native reactive tendencies,—the impulses and instincts of childhood,—so as to be able to substitute one for another, and turn them on to artificial objects.

It is often said that man is distinguished from the lower animals by having a much smaller assortment of native instincts and impulses than they, but this is a great mistake. Man, of course, has not the marvellous egg-laying instincts which some articulates have; but, if we compare him with the mammalia, we are forced to confess that he is appealed to by a much larger array of objects than any other mammal, that his reactions on these objects are characteristic and determinate in a very high degree. The monkeys, and especially the anthropoids, are the only beings that approach him in their analytic curiosity and width of imitativeness. His instinctive impulses, it is true, get overlaid by the secondary reactions due to his superior reasoning power; but thus man loses the *simply* instinctive demeanor. But the life of instinct is only disguised in him, not lost; and when the higher brain-functions are in abeyance, as happens in imbecility or dementia, his instincts sometimes show their presence in truly brutish ways.

I will therefore say a few words about those instinctive tendencies which are the most important from the teacher's point of view.

CHAPTER 7

What the Native Reactions Are

FIRST of all, *Fear*. Fear of punishment has always been the great weapon of the teacher, and will always, of course, retain some place in the conditions of the schoolroom. The subject is so familiar that nothing more need be said about it.

The same is true of *Love*, and the instinctive desire to please those whom we love. The teacher who succeeds in getting herself loved by the pupils will obtain results which one of a more forbidding temperament finds it impossible to secure.

Next, a word might be said about *Curiosity*. This is perhaps a rather poor term by which to designate the *impulse toward better cognition* in its full extent; but you will readily understand what I mean. Novelties in the way of sensible objects, especially if their sensational quality is bright, vivid, startling, invariably arrest the attention of the young and hold it until the desire to know more about the object is assuaged. In its higher more intellectual form, the impulse toward completer knowledge takes the character of scientific or philosophic curiosity. In both its sensational and its intellectual form the instinct is more vivacious during childhood and youth than in after life. Young children are possessed by curiosity about every new impression that assails them. It would be quite impossible for a young child to listen to a lecture for more than a few minutes, as you are now listening to me. The outside sights and sounds would inevitably carry his attention off.

46

And, for most people in middle life, the sort of intellectual effort required of the average schoolboy in mastering his Greek or Latin lesson, his algebra or physics, would be out of the question. The middle-aged citizen attends exclusively to the routine details of his business; and new truths, especially when they require involved trains of close reasoning, are no longer within the scope of his capacity.

The sensational curiosity of childhood is appealed to more particularly by certain determinate kind of objects. Material things, things that move, living things, human actions and accounts of human action, will win the attention better than anything that is more abstract. Here again comes in the advantage of the object-teaching and manual training methods. The pupil's attention is spontaneously held by any problem that involves the presentation of a new material object or of an activity on any one's part. The teacher's earliest appeals, therefore, must be through objects shown or acts performed or described. Theoretic curiosity, curiosity about the rational relations between things, can hardly be said to awake at all until adolescence is reached. The sporadic metaphysical inquiries of children as to who made God, and why they have five fingers, need hardly be counted here. But, when the theoretic instinct is once alive in the pupil, an entirely new order of pedagogic relations begins for him. Reasons, causes, abstract conceptions, suddenly grow full of zest, a fact with which all teachers are familiar. And, both in its sensible and in its rational developments, disinterested curiosity may be successfully appealed to in the child with much more certainty than in the adult, in whom this intellectual instinct has grown so torpid as usually never to awake unless it enters into association with some selfish personal interest. Of this latter point I will say more anon.

Imitation. Man has always been recognized as the imitative animal *par excellence*. And there is hardly a book on psychology, however old, which has not devoted at least one paragraph to this fact. It is strange, however, that the full scope and pregnancy of the imitative impulse in man has had to wait till the last dozen years to become adequately recognized. M. Tarde led the way in his admirably original work, "Les Lois de l'Imitation"; and in our own country Professors Royce and Baldwin have kept the ball rolling with all the energy that could be desired. Each of us is in fact what he is almost exclusively by virtue of his imitativeness. We become conscious of what we ourselves are by imitating others—the consciousness of what the others are precedes—the sense of self grows by the sense of pattern. The entire accumulated wealth of mankind—languages, arts, institutions, and sciences—is passed on from one generation to another by what Baldwin has called social heredity, each generation simply imitating the last. Into the particulars of this most fascinating chapter of psychology I have no time to go. The moment one hears Tarde's proposition uttered, however, one feels how supremely true it is. Invention, using the term most broadly, and imitation, are the two legs, so to call them, on which the human race historically has walked.

Imitation shades imperceptibly into *Emulation*. Emulation is the impulse to imitate what you see another doing, in order not to appear inferior; and it is hard to draw a sharp line between the manifestations of the two impulses, so inextricably do they mix their effects. Emulation is the very nerve of human society. Why are you, my hearers, sitting here before me? If no one whom you ever heard of had attended a 'summer school' or teachers' institute, would it have occurred to any one of you to break out independently and do a thing so unprescribed by fashion? Probably not. Nor would your pupils come to you unless the children of their parents' neighbors were all simultaneously being sent to school. We wish not to be lonely or eccentric, and we wish not to be cut off from our share in things which to our neighbors seem desirable privileges.

In the schoolroom, imitation and emulation play absolutely vital parts. Every teacher knows the advantage of having certain things performed by whole bands of children at a time. The teacher who meets with most success is the teacher whose own ways are the most imitable. A teacher should never try to make the pupils do a thing which she cannot do herself. "Come and let me show you how" is an incomparably better stimulus than "Go and do it as the book directs." Children admire a teacher who has skill. What he does seems easy, and they wish to emulate it. It is useless for a dull and devitalized teacher to exhort her pupils to wake up and take an interest. She must first take one herself; then her example is effective as no exhortation can possibly be.

Every school has its tone, moral and intellectual. And this tone is a mere tradition kept up by imitation, due in the first instance to the example set by teachers and by previous pupils of an aggressive and dominating type, copied by the others, and passed on from year to year, so that the new pupils take the cue almost immediately. Such a tone changes very slowly, if at all; and then always under the modifying influence of new personalities aggressive enough in character to set new patterns and not merely to copy the old. The classic example of this sort of tone is the often quoted case of Rugby under Dr. Arnold's administration. He impressed his own character as a model on the imagination of the oldest boys, who in turn were expected and required to impress theirs upon the younger set. The contagiousness of Arnold's genius was such that a Rugby man was said to be recognizable all through life by a peculiar turn of character which he acquired at school. It is obvious that psychology as such can give in this field no precepts of detail. As in so many other fields of teaching, success depends mainly on the native genius of the teacher, the sympathy, tact, and perception which enable him to seize the right moment and to set the right example.

Among the recent modern reforms of teaching methods, a certain disparagement of emulation, as a laudable spring of action in the schoolroom, has often made itself heard. More than a century ago, Rousseau, in his 'Émile,' branded rivalry between one pupil and another as too base a passion to play a part in an ideal education. "Let Émile," he said, "never be led to compare himself to other children. No rivalries, not even in running, as soon as he begins to have the power of reason. It were a hundred times better that he should not learn at all what he could only learn through jealousy or vanity. But I would mark out every year the progress he may have made, and I would compare it with the progress of the following years. I would say to him: 'You are now grown so many inches taller; there is the ditch which you jumped over, there is the burden which you raised. There is the distance to which you could throw a pebble, there the distance you could run over without losing breath. See how much more you can do now!' Thus I should excite him without making him jealous of any one. He would wish to surpass himself. I can see no inconvenience in this emulation with his former self."

Unquestionably, emulation with one's former self is a noble form of the passion of rivalry, and has a wide scope in the training of the young. But to veto and taboo all possible rivalry of one youth with another, because such rivalry may degenerate into greedy and selfish excess, does seem to savor somewhat of sentimentality, or even of fanaticism. The feeling of rivalry lies at the very basis of our being, all social improvement being largely due to it. There is a noble and generous kind of rivalry, as well as a spiteful and greedy kind; and the noble and generous form is particularly common in childhood. All games owe the zest which they bring with them to the fact that they are rooted in the emulous passion, yet they are the chief means of training in fairness and magnanimity. Can the teacher afford to throw such an ally away? Ought we seriously to hope that marks, distinctions, prizes, and other goals of effort, based on the pursuit of recognized superiority, should be forever banished from our schools? As a psychologist, obliged to notice the deep and pervasive character of the emulous passion, I must confess my doubts.

The wise teacher will use this instinct as he uses others, reaping its advantages, and appealing to it in such a way as to reap a maximum of benefit with a minimum of harm; for, after all, we must confess, with a French critic of Rousseau's doctrine, that the deepest spring of action in us is the sight of action in another. The spectacle of effort is what awakens and sustains our own effort. No runner running all alone on a race-track will find in his own will the power of stimulation which his rivalry with other runners incites, when he feels them at his heels, about to pass. When a trotting horse is 'speeded,' a running horse must go beside him to keep him to the pace.

As imitation slides into emulation, so emulation slides into *Ambition*; and ambition connects itself closely with *Pugnacity* and *Pride*. Consequently, these five instinctive tendencies form an interconnected group of factors, hard to separate in the determination of a great deal of our conduct. The *Ambitious Impulses* would perhaps be the best name for the whole group.

Pride and pugnacity have often been considered unworthy passions to appeal to in the young. But in their more refined and noble forms they play a great part in the schoolroom and in education generally, being in some characters most potent spurs to effort. Pugnacity need not be thought of merely in the form of physical combativeness. It can be taken in the sense of a general unwillingness to be beaten by any kind of difficulty. It is what makes us feel 'stumped' and challenged by arduous achievements, and is essential to a spirited and enterprising character. We have of late been hearing much of the philosophy of tenderness in education; 'interest' must be assiduously awakened in everything, difficulties must be smoothed away. *Soft* pedagogics have taken the place of the old steep and rocky path to learning. But from this lukewarm air the bracing oxygen of effort is left out. It is nonsense to suppose that every step in education *can* be interesting. The fighting impulse must often be appealed to. Make the pupil feel ashamed of being scared at fractions, of being 'downed' by the law of falling bodies; rouse his pugnacity and pride, and he will rush at the difficult places with a sort of inner wrath at himself that is one of his best moral faculties. A victory scored under such conditions becomes a turning-point and crisis of his character. It represents the high-water mark of his powers, and serves thereafter as an ideal pattern for his self-imitation. The teacher who never rouses this sort of pugnacious excitement in his pupils falls short of one of his best forms of usefulness.

The next instinct which I shall mention is that of *Ownership*, also one of the radical endowments of the race. It often is the antagonist of imitation. Whether social progress is due more to the passion for keeping old things and habits or to the passion of imitating and acquiring new ones may in some cases be a difficult thing to decide. The sense of ownership begins in the second year of life. Among the first words which an infant learns to utter are the words 'my' and 'mine,' and woe to the parents of twins who fail to provide their gifts in duplicate. The depth and primitiveness of this instinct would seem to cast a sort of psychological discredit in advance upon all radical forms of communistic utopia. Private proprietorship cannot be practically abolished until human nature is changed. It seems essential to mental health that the individual should have something beyond the bare clothes on his back to which he can assert exclusive possession, and which he may defend adversely against the world. Even those religious orders who make the most stringent vows of poverty have found it necessary to relax the rule a little in favor of the human heart made unhappy by reduction to too disinterested terms. The monk must have his books: the nun must have her little garden, and the images and pictures in her room.

In education, the instinct of ownership is fundamental, and can be appealed to in many ways. In the house, training in order and neatness begins with the arrangement of the child's own personal possessions. In the school, ownership is particularly important in connection with one of its special forms of activity, the collecting impulse. An object possibly not very interesting in itself, like a shell, a postage stamp, or a single map or drawing, will acquire an interest if it fills a gap in a collection or helps to complete a series. Much of the scholarly work of the world, so far as it is mere bibliography, memory, and erudition (and this lies at the basis of all our human scholarship), would seem to owe its interest rather to the way in which it gratifies the accumulating and collecting instinct than to any special appeal which it makes to our cravings after rationality. A man wishes a complete collection of information, wishes to know more about a subject than anybody else, much as another may wish to own more dollars or more early editions or more engravings before the letter than anybody else.

The teacher who can work this impulse into the school tasks is fortunate. Almost all children collect something. A tactful teacher may get them to take pleasure in collecting books; in keeping a neat and orderly collection of notes; in starting, when they are mature enough, a card catalogue; in preserving every drawing or map which they may make. Neatness, order, and method are thus instinctively gained, along with the other benefits which the possession of the collection entails. Even such a noisome thing as a collection of postage stamps may be used by the teacher as an inciter of interest in the geographical and historical information which she desires to impart. Sloyd successfully avails itself of this instinct in causing the pupil to make a collection of wooden implements fit for his own private use at home. Collecting is, of course, the basis of all natural history study; and probably nobody ever became a good naturalist who was not an unusually active collector when a boy.

Constructiveness is another great instinctive tendency with which the schoolroom has to contract an alliance. Up to the eighth or ninth year of childhood one may say that the child does hardly anything else than handle objects, explore things with his hands, doing and undoing, setting up and knocking down, putting together and pulling apart; for, from the psychological point of view, construction and destruction are two names for the same manual activity. Both signify the production of change, and the working of effects, in outward things. The result of all this is that intimate familiarity with the physical environment, that acquaintance with the properties of material things, which is really the foundation of human *consciousness*. To the very last, in most of us, the conceptions of objects and their properties are limited to the notion of what we can *do with them*. A 'stick' means something we can lean upon or strike with; 'fire,' something to cook, or warm ourselves, or burn things up withal; 'string,' something with which to tie things together. For most people these objects have no other meaning. In geometry, the cylinder, circle, sphere, are defined as what you get by going through certain processes of construction, revolving a parallelogram upon one of its sides, etc. The more different kinds of things a child thus gets to know by treating and handling them, the more confident grows his sense of kinship with the world in which he lives. An unsympathetic adult will wonder at the fascinated hours which a child will spend in putting his blocks together and rearranging them. But the wise education takes the tide at the flood, and from the kindergarten upward devotes the first years of education to training in construction and to object-teaching. I need not recapitulate here what I said awhile back about the superiority of the objective and experimental methods. They occupy the pupil in a way most congruous with the spontaneous interests of his age. They absorb him, and leave impressions durable and profound. Compared with the youth taught by these methods, one brought up exclusively by books carries through life a certain remoteness from reality: he stands, as it were, out of the pale, and feels that he stands so; and often suffers a kind of melancholy from which he might have been rescued by a more real education.

There are other impulses, such as love of approbation or vanity, shyness and secretiveness, of which a word might be said; but they are too familiar to need it. You can easily pursue the subject by your own reflection. There is one general law, however, that relates to many of our instinctive tendencies, and that has no little importance in education; and I must refer to it briefly before I leave the subject. It has been called the law of transitoriness in instincts. Many of our impulsive tendencies ripen at a certain period; and, if the appropriate objects be then and there provided, habits of conduct toward them are acquired which last. But, if the objects be not forthcoming then, the impulse may die out before a habit is formed; and later it may be hard to teach the creature to react appropriately in those directions. The sucking instincts in mammals, the following instinct in certain birds and quadrupeds, are examples of this: they fade away shortly after birth.

In children we observe a ripening of impulses and interests in a certain determinate order. Creeping, walking, climbing, imitating vocal sounds, constructing, drawing, calculating, possess the child in succession; and in some children the possession, while it lasts, may be of a semi-frantic and exclusive sort. Later the interest in any one of these things may wholly fade away. Of course, the proper pedagogic moment to work skill in, and to clench the useful habit, is when the native impulse is most acutely present. Crowd on the athletic opportunities, the mental arithmetic, the verse-learning, the drawing, the botany, or what not, the moment you have reason to think the hour is ripe. The hour may not last long, and while it continues you may safely let all the child's other occupations take a second place. In this way you economize time and deepen skill; for many an infant prodigy, artistic or mathematical, has a flowering epoch of but a few months.

One can draw no specific rules for all this. It depends on close observation in the particular case, and parents here have a great advantage over teachers. In fact, the law of transitoriness has little chance of individualized application in the schools.

Such is the little interested and impulsive psychophysical organism whose springs of action the teacher must divine, and to whose ways he must become accustomed.

He must start with the native tendencies, and enlarge the pupil's entire passive and active experience. He must ply him with new objects and stimuli, and make him taste the fruits of his behavior, so that now that whole context of remembered experience is what shall determine his conduct when he gets the stimulus, and not the bare immediate impression. As the pupil's life thus enlarges, it gets fuller and fuller of all sorts of memories and associations and substitutions; but the eye accustomed to psychological analysis will discern, underneath it all, the outlines of our simple psychophysical scheme.

Respect then, I beg you, always the original reactions, even when you are seeking to overcome their connection with certain objects, and to supplant them with others that you wish to make the rule. Bad behavior, from the point of view of the teacher's art, is as good a starting-point as good behavior. In fact, paradoxical as it may sound to say so, it is often a better starting-point than good behavior would be.

The acquired reactions must be made habitual whenever they are appropriate. Therefore Habit is the next subject to which your attention is invited.

CHAPTER 8

The Laws of Habit

IT IS very important that teachers should realize the importance of habit, and psychology helps us greatly at this point. We speak, it is true, of good habits and of bad habits; but, when people use the word 'habit,' in the majority of instances it is a bad habit which they have in mind. They talk of the smoking-habit and the swearing-habit and the drinking-habit, but not of the abstention-habit or the moderation-habit or the courage-habit. But the fact is that our virtues are habits as much as our vices. All our life, so far as it has definite form, is but a mass of habits,—practical, emotional, and intellectual,—systematically organized for our weal or woe, and bearing us irresistibly toward our destiny, whatever the latter may be.

Since pupils can understand this at a comparatively early age, and since to understand it contributes in no small measure to their feeling of responsibility, it would be well if the teacher were able himself to talk to them of the philosophy of habit in some such abstract terms as I am now about to talk of it to you.

I believe that we are subject to the law of habit in consequence of the fact that we have bodies. The plasticity of the living matter of our nervous system, in short, is the reason why we do a thing with difficulty the first time, but soon do it more and more easily, and finally, with sufficient practice, do it semi-mechanically, or with hardly any consciousness at all. Our nervous systems have (in Dr. Carpenter's words) *grown* to the way in which they have been exercised, just as a sheet of paper or a coat, once creased or folded, tends to fall forever afterward into the same identical folds.

Habit is thus a second nature, or rather, as the Duke of Wellington said, it is 'ten times nature,'—at any rate as regards its importance in adult life; for the acquired habits of our training have by that time inhibited or strangled most of the natural impulsive tendencies which were originally there. Ninety-nine hundredths or, possibly, nine hundred and ninety-nine thousandths of our activity is purely automatic and habitual, from our rising in the morning to our lying down each night. Our dressing and undressing, our eating and drinking, our greetings and partings, our hat-raisings and giving way for ladies to precede, nay, even most of the forms of our common speech, are things of a type so fixed by repetition as almost to be classed as reflex actions. To each sort of impression we have an automatic, ready-made response. My very words to you now are an example of what I mean; for having already lectured upon habit and printed a chapter about it in a book, and read the latter when in print, I find my tongue inevitably falling into its old phrases and repeating almost literally what I said before.

So far as we are thus mere bundles of habit, we are stereotyped creatures, imitators and copiers of our past selves. And since this, under any circumstances, is what we always tend to become, it follows first of all that the teacher's prime concern should be to ingrain into the pupil that assortment of habits that shall be most useful to him throughout life. Education is for behavior, and habits are the stuff of which behavior consists.

To quote my earlier book directly, the great thing in all education is to *make our nervous system our ally instead of our enemy*. It is to fund and capitalize our acquisitions, and live at ease upon the interest of the fund. *For this we must make automatic and habitual, as early as possible, as many useful actions as we can*, and as carefully guard against the growing into ways that are likely to be dis-advantageous. The more of the details of our daily life we can hand over to the effortless custody of automatism, the more our higher powers of mind will be set free for their own proper work. There is no more miserable human being than one in whom nothing is habitual but indecision, and for whom the lighting of every cigar, the drinking of every cup, the time of rising and going to bed every day, and the beginning of every bit of work are subjects of express volitional deliberation. Full half the time of such a man goes to the deciding or regretting of matters which ought to be so ingrained in him as practically not to exist for his consciousness at all. If there be such daily duties not yet ingrained in any one of my hearers, let him begin this very hour to set the matter right.

In Professor Bain's chapter on 'The Moral Habits' there are some admirable practical remarks laid down. Two great maxims emerge from the treatment. The first is that in the acquisition of a new habit, or the leaving off of an old one, we must take care to *launch ourselves with as strong and decided an initiative as possible.* Accumulate all the possible circumstances which shall reinforce the right motives; put yourself assiduously in conditions that encourage the new way; make engagements incompatible with the old; take a public pledge, if the case allows; in short, envelop your resolution with every aid you know. This will give your new beginning such a momentum that the temptation to break down will not occur as soon as it otherwise might; and every day during which a breakdown is postponed adds to the chances of its not occurring at all.

I remember long ago reading in an Austrian paper the advertisement of a certain Rudolph Somebody, who promised fifty gulden reward to any one who after that date should find him at the wine-shop of Ambrosius So-and-so. 'This I do,' the advertisement continued, 'in consequence of a promise which I have made my wife.' With such a wife, and such an understanding of the way in which to start new habits, it would be safe to stake one's money on Rudolph's ultimate success.

The second maxim is, *Never suffer an exception to occur till the new habit is securely rooted in your life.* Each lapse is like the letting fall of a ball of string which one is carefully winding up: a single slip undoes more than a great many turns will wind again. Continuity of training is the great means of making the nervous system act infallibly right. As Professor Bain says:—

"The peculiarity of the moral habits, contradistinguishing them from the intellectual acquisitions, is the presence of two hostile powers, one to be gradually raised into the ascendant over the other. It is necessary above all things, in such a situation, never to lose a battle. Every gain on the wrong side undoes the effect of many conquests on the right. The essential precaution, therefore, is so to regulate the two opposing powers that the one may have a series of uninterrupted successes, until repetition has fortified it to such a degree as to enable it to cope with the opposition, under any circumstances. This is the theoretically best career of mental progress."

A third maxim may be added to the preceding pair: *Seize the very first possible opportunity to act on every resolution you make, and on every emotional prompting you may experience in the direction of the habits you aspire to gain.* It is not in the moment of their forming, but in the moment of their producing motor effects, that resolves and aspirations communicate the new 'set' to the brain.

No matter how full a reservoir of maxims one may possess, and no matter how good one's sentiments may be, if one have not taken advantage of every concrete opportunity to act, one's character may remain entirely unaffected for the better. With good intentions, hell proverbially is paved. This is an obvious consequence of the principles I have laid down. A 'character,' as J. S. Mill says, 'is a completely fashioned will'; and a will, in the sense in which he means it, is an aggregate of tendencies to act in a firm and prompt and definite way upon all the principal emergencies of life. A tendency to act only becomes effectively ingrained in us in proportion to the uninterrupted frequency with which the actions actually occur, and the brain 'grows' to their use. When a resolve or a fine glow of feeling is allowed to evaporate without bearing practical fruit, it is worse than a chance lost: it works so as positively to hinder future resolutions and emotions from taking the normal path of discharge. There is no more contemptible type of human character than that of the nerveless sentimentalist and dreamer, who spends his life in a weltering sea of sensibility, but never does a concrete manly deed.

This leads to a fourth maxim. *Don't preach too much to your pupils or abound in good talk in the abstract.* Lie in wait rather for the practical opportunities, be prompt to seize those as they pass, and thus at one operation get your pupils both to think, to feel, and to do. The strokes of *behavior* are what give the new set to the character, and work the good habits into its organic tissue. Preaching and talking too soon become an ineffectual bore.

There is a passage in Darwin's short autobiography which has been often quoted, and which, for the sake of its bearing on our subject of habit, I must now quote again. Darwin says: "Up to the age of thirty or beyond it, poetry of many kinds gave me great pleasure; and even as a schoolboy I took intense delight in Shakespeare, especially in the historical plays. I have also said that pictures formerly gave me considerable, and music very great delight. But now for many years I cannot endure to read a line of poetry. I have tried lately to read Shakespeare, and found it so intolerably dull that it nauseated me. I have also almost lost my taste for pictures or music. . . . My mind seems to have become a kind of machine for grinding general laws out of large collections of facts; but why this should have caused the atrophy of that part of the brain alone, on which the higher tastes depend, I cannot conceive. . . . If I had to live my life again, I would have made a rule to read some poetry and listen to some music at least once every week; for perhaps the parts of my brain now atrophied would thus have been kept alive through use. The loss of these tastes is a loss of happiness, and may possibly be injurious to the intellect, and more probably to the moral character, by enfeebling the emotional part of our nature."

We all intend when young to be all that may become a man, before the destroyer cuts us down. We wish and expect to enjoy poetry always, to grow more and more intelligent about pictures and music, to keep in touch with spiritual and religious ideas, and even not to let the greater philosophic thoughts of our time develop quite beyond our view. We mean all this in youth, I say; and yet in how many middle-aged men and women is such an honest and sanguine expectation fulfilled? Surely, in comparatively few; and the laws of habit show us why. Some interest in each of these things arises in everybody at the proper age; but, if not persistently fed with the appropriate matter, instead of growing into a powerful and necessary habit, it atrophies and dies, choked by the rival interests to which the daily food is given. We make ourselves into Darwins in this negative respect by persistently ignoring the essential practical conditions of our case. We say abstractly: "I mean to enjoy poetry, and to absorb a lot of it, of course. I fully intend to keep up my love of music, to read the books that shall give new turns to the thought of my time, to keep my higher spiritual side alive, etc." But we do not attack these things concretely, and we do not begin *to-day*. We forget that every good that is worth possessing must be paid for in strokes of daily effort. We postpone and postpone, until those smiling possibilities are dead. Whereas ten minutes a day of poetry, of spiritual reading or meditation, and an hour or two a week at music, pictures, or philosophy, provided we began *now* and suffered no remission, would infallibly give us in due time the fulness of all we desire. By neglecting the necessary concrete labor, by sparing ourselves the little daily tax, we are positively digging the graves of our higher possibilities. This is a point concerning which you teachers might well give a little timely information to your older and more aspiring pupils.

According as a function receives daily exercise or not, the man becomes a different kind of being in later life. We have lately had a number of accomplished Hindoo visitors at Cambridge, who talked freely of life and philosophy. More than one of them has confided to me that the sight of our faces, all contracted as they are with the habitual American over-intensity and anxiety of expression, and our ungraceful and distorted attitudes when sitting, made on him a very painful impression. "I do not see," said one, "how it is possible for you to live as you do, without a single minute in your day deliberately given to tranquillity and meditation. It is an invariable part of our Hindoo life to retire for at least half an hour daily into silence, to relax our muscles, govern our breathing, and meditate on eternal things. Every Hindoo child is trained to this from a very early age." The good fruits of such a discipline were obvious in the physical repose and lack of tension, and the wonderful smoothness and calmness of facial expression, and imperturbability of manner of these Orientals. I felt that my countrymen were depriving themselves of an essential grace of character. How many American children ever hear it said by parent or teacher, that they should moderate their piercing voices, that they should relax their unused muscles, and as far as possible, when sitting, sit quite still? Not one in a thousand, not one in five thousand! Yet, from its reflex influence on the inner mental states, this ceaseless over-tension, over-motion, and over-expression are working on us grievous national harm.

I beg you teachers to think a little seriously of this matter. Perhaps you can help our rising generation of Americans toward the beginning of a better set of personal ideals.*

To go back now to our general maxims, I may at last, as a fifth and final practical maxim about habits, offer something like this: *Keep the faculty of effort alive in you by a little gratuitous exercise every day.* That is, be systematically heroic in little unnecessary points, do every day or two something for no other reason than its difficulty, so that, when the hour of dire need draws nigh, it may find you not unnerved and untrained to stand the test. Asceticism of this sort is like the insurance which a man pays on his house and goods. The tax does him no good at the time, and possibly may never bring him a return. But, if the fire *does* come, his having paid it will be his salvation from ruin. So with the man who has daily inured himself to habits of concentrated attention, energetic volition, and self-denial in unnecessary things. He will stand like a tower when everything rocks around

* See the Address on the Gospel of Relaxation, later in this volume.

him, and his softer fellow-mortals are winnowed like chaff in the blast.

I have been accused, when talking of the subject of habit, of making old habits appear so strong that the acquiring of new ones, and particularly anything like a sudden reform or conversion, would be made impossible by my doctrine. Of course, this would suffice to condemn the latter; for sudden conversions, however infrequent they may be, unquestionably do occur. But there is no incompatibility between the general laws I have laid down and the most startling sudden alterations in the way of character. New habits *can* be launched, I have expressly said, on condition of there being new stimuli and new excitements. Now life abounds in these, and sometimes they are such critical and revolutionary experiences that they change a man's whole scale of values and system of ideas. In such cases, the old order of his habits will be ruptured; and, if the new motives are lasting, new habits will be formed, and build up in him a new or regenerate 'nature.'

All this kind of fact I fully allow. But the general laws of habit are no wise altered thereby, and the physiological study of mental conditions still remains on the whole the most powerful ally of hortatory ethics. The hell to be endured hereafter, of which theology tells, is no worse than the hell we make for ourselves in this world by habitually fashioning our characters in the wrong way. Could the young but realize how soon they will become mere walking bundles of habits, they would give more heed to their conduct while in the plastic state. We are spinning our own fates, good or evil, and never to be undone. Every smallest stroke of virtue or of vice leaves its never-so-little scar. The drunken Rip Van Winkle, in Jefferson's play, excuses himself for every fresh dereliction by saying, "I won't count this time!" Well, he may not count it, and a kind Heaven may not count it; but it is being counted none the less. Down among his nerve-cells and fibres the molecules are counting it, registering and storing it up to be used against him when the next temptation comes.

Nothing we ever do is, in strict scientific literalness, wiped out.

Of course, this has its good side as well as its bad one. As we become permanent drunkards by so many separate drinks, so we become saints in the moral, and authorities and experts in the practical and scientific spheres, by so many separate acts and hours of work. Let no youth have any anxiety about the upshot of his education, whatever the line of it may be. If he keep faithfully busy each hour of the working day, he may safely leave the final result to itself. He can with perfect certainty count on waking up some fine morning to find himself one of the competent ones of his generation, in whatever pursuit he may have singled out. Silently, between all the details of his business, the *power of judging* in all that class of matter will have built itself up within him as a possession that will never pass away. Young people should know this truth in advance. The ignorance of it has probably engendered more discouragement and faint-heartedness in youths embarking on arduous careers than all other causes put together.

CHAPTER 9

The Association of Ideas

IN MY last talk, in treating of Habit, I chiefly had in mind our *motor* habits,—habits of external conduct. But our thinking and feeling processes are also largely subject to the law of habit, and one result of this is a phenomenon which you all know under the name of 'the association of ideas.' To that phenomenon I ask you now to turn.

You remember that consciousness is an ever-flowing

stream of objects, feelings, and impulsive tendencies. We saw already that its phases or pulses are like so many fields or waves, each field or wave having usually its central point of liveliest attention, in the shape of the most prominent object in our thought, while all around this lies a margin of other objects more dimly realized, together with the margin of emotional and active tendencies which the whole entails. Describing the mind thus in fluid terms, we cling as close as possible to nature. At first sight, it might seem as if, in the fluidity of these successive waves, everything is indeterminate. But inspection shows that each wave has a constitution which can be to some degree explained by the constitution of the waves just passed away. And this relation of the wave to its predecessors is expressed by the two fundamental 'laws of association,' so-called, of which the first is named the Law of Contiguity, the second that of Similarity.

The *Law of Contiguity* tells us that objects thought of in the coming wave are such as in some previous experience were *next* to the objects represented in the wave that is passing away. The vanishing objects were once formerly their neighbors in the mind. When you recite the alphabet or your prayers, or when the sight of an object reminds you of its name, or the name reminds you of the object, it is through the law of contiguity that the terms are suggested to the mind.

The *Law of Similarity* says that, when contiguity fails to describe what happens, the coming objects will prove to *resemble* the going objects, even though the two were never experienced together before. In our 'flights of fancy,' this is frequently the case.

If, arresting ourselves in the flow of reverie, we ask the question, "How came we to be thinking of just this object now?" we can almost always trace its presence to some previous object which has introduced it to the mind, according to one or the other of these laws. The entire routine of our memorized acquisitions, for example, is a consequence of nothing but the Law of Contiguity. The words of a poem, the formulas of trigonometry, the facts of history, the properties of material things, are all known to us as definite systems or groups of objects which cohere in an order fixed by innumerable iterations, and of which any one part reminds us of the others. In dry and prosaic minds, almost all the mental sequences flow along these lines of habitual routine repetition and suggestion.

In witty, imaginative minds, on the other hand, the routine is broken through with ease at any moment; and one field of mental objects will suggest another with which perhaps in the whole history of human thinking it had never once before been coupled. The link here is usually some *analogy* between the objects successively thought of,—an analogy often so subtle that, although we feel it, we can with difficulty analyze its ground; as where, for example, we find something masculine in the color red and something feminine in the color pale blue, or where, of three human beings' characters, one will remind us of a cat, another of a dog, the third perhaps of a cow.

Psychologists have of course gone very deeply into the question of what the causes of association may be; and some of them have tried to show that contiguity and similarity are not two radically diverse laws, but that either presupposes the presence of the other. I myself am disposed to think that the phenomena of association depend on our cerebral constitution, and are not immediate consequences of our being rational beings. In other words, when we shall have become disembodied spirits, it may be that our trains of consciousness will follow different laws. These questions are discussed in the books on psychology, and I hope that some of you will be interested in following them there. But I will, on the present occasion, ignore them entirely; for, as teachers, it is the *fact* of association that practically concerns you, let its grounds be spiritual or cerebral, or what they may, and let its laws be reducible, or non-reducible, to one. Your pupils, whatever else they are, are at any rate little pieces of associating machinery. Their education consists in the organizing within them of determinate tendencies to associate one thing with another,—impressions with consequences, these with reactions, those with results, and so on indefinitely. The more copious the associative systems, the completer the individual's adaptations to the world.

The teacher can formulate his function to himself therefore in terms of 'association' as well as in terms of 'native and acquired reaction.' It is mainly that of *building up useful systems of association* in the pupil's mind. This description sounds wider than the one I began by giving. But, when one thinks that our trains of association, whatever they may be, normally issue in acquired reactions or behavior, one sees that in a general way the same mass of facts is covered by both formulas.

It is astonishing how many mental operations we can explain when we have once grasped the principles of association. The great problem which association undertakes to solve is, *Why does just this particular field of consciousness, constituted in this particular way, now appear before my mind?* It may be a field of objects imagined; it may be of objects remembered or of objects perceived; it may include an action resolved on. In either case, when the field is analyzed into its parts, those parts can be shown to have proceeded from parts of fields previously before consciousness, in consequence of one or other of the laws of association just laid down. Those laws *run* the mind: interest, shifting hither and thither, deflects it; and attention, as we shall later see, steers it and keeps it from too zigzag a course.

To grasp these factors clearly gives one a solid and simple understanding of the psychological machinery. The 'nature,' the 'character,' of an individual means really nothing but the habitual form of his associations. To break up bad associations or wrong ones, to build others in, to guide the associative tendencies into the most fruitful channels, is the educator's principal task. But here, as with all other simple principles, the difficulty lies in the application. Psychology can state the laws: concrete tact and talent alone can work them to useful results.

Meanwhile it is a matter of the commonest experience

that our minds may pass from one object to another by various intermediary fields of consciousness. The inde· terminateness of our paths of association *in concreto* is thus almost as striking a feature of them as the uniformity of their abstract form. Start from any idea whatever, and the entire range of your ideas is potentially at your disposal. If we take as the associative starting-point, or cue, some simple word which I pronounce before you, there is no limit to the possible diversity of suggestions which it may set up in your minds. Suppose I say 'blue,' for example: some of you may think of the blue sky and hot weather from which we now are suffering, then go off on thoughts of summer clothing, or possibly of meteorology at large; others may think of the spectrum and the physiology of color-vision, and glide into X-rays and recent physical speculations; others may think of blue ribbons, or of the blue flowers on a friend's hat, and proceed on lines of personal reminiscence. To others, again, etymology and linguistic thoughts may be suggested; or blue may be 'apperceived' as a synonym for melancholy, and a train of associates connected with morbid psychology may proceed to unroll themselves.

In the same person, the same word heard at different times will provoke, in consequence of the varying marginal preoccupations, either one of a number of diverse possible associative sequences. Professor Münsterberg performed this experiment methodically, using the same words four times over, at three-month intervals, as 'cues' for four different persons who were the subjects of observation. He found almost no constancy in their associations taken at these different times. In short, the entire potential content of one's consciousness is accessible from any one of its points. This is why we can never work the laws of association forward: starting from the present field as a cue, we can never cipher out in advance just what the person will be thinking of five minutes later. The elements which may become prepotent in the process, the parts of each successive field round which the associations shall chiefly turn, the possible bifurcations of suggestion, are so numerous and ambiguous as to be indeterminable before the fact. But, although we cannot work the laws of. association forward, we can always work them backwards. We cannot say now what we shall find ourselves thinking of five minutes hence; but, whatever it may be, we shall then be able to trace it through intermediary links of contiguity or similarity to what we are thinking now. What so baffles our prevision is the shifting part played by the margin and focus—in fact, by each element by itself of the margin or focus—in calling up the next ideas.

For example, I am reciting 'Locksley Hall,' in order to divert my mind from a state of suspense that I am in concerning the will of a relative that is dead. The will still remains in the mental background as an extremely marginal or ultramarginal portion of my field of consciousness; but the poem fairly keeps my attention from it, until I come to the line, "I, the heir of all the ages, in the foremost files of time." The words 'I, the heir,' immediately make an electric connection with the marginal thought of the will; that, in turn, makes my heart beat with anticipation of my possible legacy, so that I throw down the book and pace the floor excitedly with visions of my future fortune pouring through my mind. Any portion of the field of consciousness that has more potentialities of emotional excitement than another may thus be roused to predominant activity; and the shifting play of interest now in one portion, now in another, deflects the currents in all sorts of zigzag ways, the mental activity running hither and thither as the sparks run in burnt-up paper.

One more point, and I shall have said as much to you as seems necessary about the process of association.

You just saw how a single exciting word may call up its own associates prepotently, and deflect our whole train of thinking from the previous track. The fact is that every portion of the field *tends* to call up its own associates; but, if these associates be severally different, there is rivalry, and as soon as one or a few begin to be effective the others seem to get siphoned out, as it were, and left behind. Seldom, however, as in our example, does the process seem to turn round a single item in the mental field, or even round the entire field that is immediately in the act of passing. It is a matter of *constellation*, into which portions of fields that are already past especially seem to enter and have their say. Thus, to go back to 'Locksley Hall,' each word as I recite it in its due order is suggested not solely by the previous word now expiring on my lips, but it is rather the effect of all the previous words, taken together, of the verse. "Ages," for example, calls up "in the foremost files of time," when preceded by "I, the heir of all the"—; but, when preceded by "for I doubt not through the,"—it calls up "one increasing purpose runs." Similarly, if I write on the blackboard the letters A B C D E F, . . . they probably suggest to you G H I. . . . But if I write A B A D D E F, if they suggest anything, they suggest as their complement E C T or E F I C I E N C Y. The result depending on the total constellation, even though most of the single items be the same.

My practical reason for mentioning this law is this, that it follows from it that, in working associations into your pupils' minds, you must not rely on single cues, but multiply the cues as much as possible. Couple the desired reaction with numerous constellations of antecedents,—don't always ask the question, for example, in the same way; don't use the same kind of data in numerical problems; vary your illustrations, etc., as much as you can. When we come to the subject of memory, we shall learn still more about this.

So much, then, for the general subject of association. In leaving it for other topics (in which, however, we shall abundantly find it involved again), I cannot too strongly urge you to acquire a habit of thinking of your pupils in associative terms. All governors of mankind, from doctors and jail-wardens to demagogues and statesmen, instinctively come so to conceive their charges. If you do the same, thinking of them (however else you may think of them besides) as so many little systems of associating machinery, you will be astonished at the intimacy of insight into their operations and at the practicality of the results which you will gain. We think of our acquaintances, for example, as characterized by certain 'tendencies.' These tendencies will in almost every instance prove to be tendencies to association. Certain ideas in them are always followed by certain other ideas, these by certain feelings and impulses to approve or disapprove, assent or decline. If the topic arouse one of those first ideas, the practical outcome can be pretty well foreseen. 'Types of character' in short are largely types of association.

CHAPTER 10

Interest

AT OUR last meeting I treated of the native tendencies of the pupil to react in characteristically definite ways upon different stimuli or exciting circumstances. In fact, I treated of the pupil's instincts. Now some situations appeal to special instincts from the very outset, and others fail to do so until the proper connections have been organized in the course of the person's training. We say of the former set of objects or situations that they are *interesting* in themselves and originally. Of the latter we say that they are natively uninteresting, and that interest in them has first to be acquired.

No topic has received more attention from pedagogical writers than that of interest. It is the natural sequel to the instincts we so lately discussed, and it is therefore well fitted to be the next subject which we take up.

Since some objects are natively interesting and in others interest is artificially acquired, the teacher must know which the natively interesting ones are; for, as we shall see immediately, other objects can artificially acquire an interest only through first becoming associated with some of these natively interesting things.

The native interests of children lie altogether in the sphere of sensation. Novel things to look at or novel sounds to hear, especially when they involve the spectacle of action of a violent sort, will always divert the attention from abstract conceptions of objects verbally taken in. The grimace that Johnny is making, the spitballs that Tommy is ready to throw, the dog-fight in the street, or the distant firebells ringing,—these are the rivals with which the teacher's powers of being interesting have incessantly to cope. The child will always attend more to what a teacher does than to what the same teacher says. During the performance of experiments or while the teacher is drawing on the blackboard, the children are tranquil and absorbed. I have seen a roomful of college students suddenly become perfectly still, to look at their professor of physics tie a piece of string around a stick which he was going to use in an experiment, but immediately grow restless when he began to explain the experiment. A lady told me that one day, during a lesson, she was delighted at having captured so completely the attention of one of her young charges. He did not remove his eyes from her face; but he said to her after the lesson was over, "I looked at you all the time, and your upper jaw did not move once!" That was the only fact that he had taken in.

Living things, then, moving things, or things that savor of danger or of blood, that have a dramatic quality,— these are the objects natively interesting to childhood, to the exclusion of almost everything else; and the teacher of young children, until more artificial interests have grown up, will keep in touch with her pupils by constant appeal to such matters as these. Instruction must be carried on objectively, experimentally, anecdotally. The blackboard-drawing and story-telling must constantly come in. But of course these methods cover only the first steps, and carry one but a little way.

Can we now formulate any general principle by which the later and more artificial interests connect themselves with these early ones that the child brings with him to the school?

Fortunately, we can: there is a very simple law that relates the acquired and the native interests with each other.

Any object not interesting in itself may become interesting through becoming associated with an object in which an interest already exists. The two associated objects grow, as it were, together: the interesting portion sheds its quality over the whole; and thus things not interesting in their own right borrow an interest which becomes as real and as strong as that of any natively interesting thing. The odd circumstance is that the borrowing does not impoverish the source, the objects taken together being more interesting, perhaps, than the originally interesting portion was by itself.

This is one of the most striking proofs of the range of application of the principle of association of ideas in psychology. An idea will infect another with its own emotional interest when they have become both associated together into any sort of a mental total. As there is no limit to the various associations into which an interesting idea may enter, one sees in how many ways an interest may be derived.

You will understand this abstract statement easily if I take the most frequent of concrete examples,—the interest which things borrow from their connection with our own personal welfare. The most natively interesting object to a man is his own personal self and its fortunes. We accordingly see that the moment a thing becomes connected with the fortunes of the self, it forthwith becomes an interesting thing. Lend the child his books, pencils, and other apparatus: then give them to him, make them his own, and notice the new light with which they instantly shine in his eyes. He takes a new kind of care of them altogether.

In mature life, all the drudgery of a man's business or profession, intolerable in itself, is shot through with engrossing significance because he knows it to be associated with his personal fortunes. What more deadly uninteresting object can there be than a railroad time-table? Yet where will you find a more interesting object if you are going on a journey, and by its means can find your train? At such times the time-table will absorb a man's entire attention, its interest being borrowed solely from its relation to his personal life. *From all these facts there emerges a very simple abstract programme for the teacher to follow in keeping the attention of the child: Begin with the line of his native interests, and offer him objects that have some immediate connection with these.* The kindergarten methods, the object-teaching routine, the blackboard and manual-training work, —all recognize this feature. Schools in which these methods preponderate are schools where discipline is easy, and where the voice of the master claiming order and attention in threatening tones need never be heard.

Next, step by step, connect with these first objects and experiences the later objects and ideas which you wish to instill. Associate the new with the old in some natural and telling way, so that the interest, being shed along from point to point, finally suffuses the entire system of objects of thought.

This is the abstract statement; and, abstractly, nothing can be easier to understand. It is in the fulfilment of the rule that the difficulty lies; for the difference between an interesting and a tedious teacher consists in little more than the inventiveness by which the one is able to mediate these associations and connections, and in the dulness in discovering such transitions which the other shows. One teacher's mind will fairly coruscate with points of connection between the new lesson and the circumstances of the children's other experience. Anecdotes and reminiscences will abound in her talk; and the shuttle of interest will shoot backward and forward, weaving the new and the old together in a lively and entertaining way. Another teacher has no such inventive fertility, and his lesson will always be a dead and heavy thing. This is the psychological meaning of the Herbartian principle of 'preparation' for each lesson, and of correlating the new with the old. It is the psychological meaning of that whole method of concentration in studies of which you have been recently hearing so much. When the geography and English and history and arithmetic simultaneously make cross-references to one another, you get an interesting set of processes all along the line.

If, then, you wish to insure the interest of your pupils, there is only one way to do it; and that is to make certain that they have something in their minds *to attend with*, when you begin to talk. That something can consist in nothing but a previous lot of ideas already interesting in themselves, and of such a nature that the incoming novel objects which you present can dovetail into them and form with them some kind of a logically associated or systematic whole. Fortunately, almost any kind of a connection is sufficient to carry the interest along. What a help is our Philippine war at present in teaching geography! But before the war you could ask the children if they ate pepper with their eggs, and where they supposed the pepper came from. Or ask them if glass is a stone, and, if not, why not; and then let them know how stones are formed and glass manufactured. External links will serve as well as those that are deeper and more logical. But interest, once shed upon a subject, is liable to remain always with that subject. Our acquisitions become in a measure portions of our personal self; and little by little, as cross-associations multiply and habits of familiarity and practice grow, the entire system of our objects of thought consolidates, most of it becoming interesting for some purposes and in some degree.

An adult man's interests are almost every one of them intensely artificial: they have slowly been built up. The objects of professional interest are most of them, in their original nature, repulsive; but by their connection with such natively exciting objects as one's personal fortune, one's social responsibilities, and especially by the force of inveterate habit, they grow to be the only things for which in middle life a man profoundly cares. But in all these the spread and consolidation have followed nothing but the principles first laid down. If we could recall for a moment our whole individual history, we should see that our professional ideals and the zeal they inspire are due to nothing but the slow accretion of one mental object to another, traceable backward from point to point till we reach the moment when, in the nursery or in the schoolroom, some little story told, some little object shown, some little operation witnessed, brought the first new object and new interest within our ken by associating it with some one of those primitively there. The interest now suffusing the whole system took its rise in that little event, so insignificant to us now as to be entirely forgotten. As the bees in swarming cling to one another in layers till the few are reached whose feet grapple the bough from which the swarm depends; so with the objects of our thinking,—they hang to each other by associated links, but the·*original* source of interest in all of them is the native interest which the earliest one once possessed.

CHAPTER 11

Attention

WHOEVER treats of interest inevitably treats of attention, for to say that an object is interesting is only another way of saying that it excites attention. But in addition to the attention which any object already interesting or just becoming interesting claims—passive attention or spontane-

ous attention, we may call it—there is a more deliberate
attention,—voluntary attention or attention with effort, as
it is called,—which we can give to objects less interesting
or uninteresting in themselves. The distinction between active and passive attention is made in all books on psychology, and connects itself with the deeper aspects of the
topic. From our present purely practical point of view, however, it is not necessary to be intricate; and passive attention to natively interesting material requires no further
elucidation on this occasion. All that we need explicitly
to note is that, the more the passive attention is relied on,
by keeping the material interesting; and the less the kind of
attention requiring effort is appealed to; the more smoothly
and pleasantly the class-room work goes on. I must say a
few more words, however, about this latter process of voluntary and deliberate attention.

One often hears it said that genius is nothing but a
power of sustained attention, and the popular impression
probably prevails that men of genius are remarkable for
their voluntary powers in this direction. *But a little introspective observation will show any one that voluntary attention cannot be continuously sustained,—that it comes in
beats.* When we are studying an uninteresting subject, if our
mind tends to wander, we have to bring back our attention
every now and then by using distinct pulses of effort, which
revivify the topic for a moment, the mind then running on
for a certain number of seconds or minutes with spontaneous interest, until again some intercurrent idea captures it
and takes it off. Then the processes of volitional recall
must be repeated once more. Voluntary attention, in short,
is only a momentary affair. The process, whatever it is, ex-
hausts itself in the single act; and, unless the matter is then
taken in hand by some trace of interest inherent in the subject, the mind fails to follow it at all. The sustained attention of the genius, sticking to his subject for hours together,
is for the most part of the passive sort. The minds of geniuses are full of copious and original associations. The subject of thought, once started, develops all sorts of fascinating consequences. The attention is led along one of these

to another in the most interesting manner, and the attention never once tends to stray away.

In a commonplace mind, on the other hand, a subject develops much less numerous associates: it dies out then quickly; and, if the man is to keep up thinking of it at all, he must bring his attention back to it by a violent wrench. In him, therefore, the faculty of voluntary attention receives abundant opportunity for cultivation in daily life. It is your despised business man, your common man of affairs, (so looked down on by the literary awarders of fame) whose virtue in this regard is likely to be most developed; for he has to listen to the concerns of so many uninteresting people, and to transact so much drudging detail, that the faculty in question is always kept in training. A genius, on the contrary, is the man in whom you are least likely to find the power of attending to anything insipid or distasteful in itself. He breaks his engagements, leaves his letters unanswered, neglects his family duties incorrigibly, because he is powerless to turn his attention down and back from those more interesting trains of imagery with which his genius constantly occupies his mind.

Voluntary attention is thus an essentially instantaneous affair. You can claim it, for your purposes in the schoolroom, by commanding it in loud, imperious tones; and you can easily get it in this way. But, unless the subject to which you thus recall their attention has inherent power to interest the pupils, you will have got it for only a brief moment; and their minds will soon be wandering again. To keep them where you have called them, you must make the subject too interesting for them to wander again. And for that there is one prescription; but the prescription, like all our prescriptions, is abstract, and, to get practical results from it, you must couple it with mother-wit.

The prescription is that *the subject must be made to show new aspects of itself; to prompt new questions; in a word, to change.* From an unchanging subject the attention inevitably wanders away. You can test this by the simplest possible case of sensorial attention. Try to attend steadfastly to a dot on the paper or on the wall. You presently find that one or the other of two things has happened: either your field of vision has become blurred, so that you now see nothing distinct at all, or else you have involuntarily ceased to look at the dot in question, and are looking at something else. But, if you ask yourself successive questions about the dot,—how big it is, how far, of what shape, what shade of color, etc.; in other words, if you turn it over, if you think of it in various ways, and along with various kinds of associates,—you can keep your mind on it for a comparatively long time. This is what the genius does, in whose hands a given topic coruscates and grows. And this is what the teacher must do for every topic if he wishes to avoid too frequent appeals to voluntary attention of the coerced sort. In all respects, reliance upon such attention as this is a wasteful method, bringing bad temper and nervous wear and tear as well as imperfect results. The teacher who can get along by keeping spontaneous interest excited must be regarded as the teacher with the greatest skill.

There is, however, in all schoolroom work a large mass of material that must be dull and unexciting, and to which it is impossible in any continuous way to contribute an interest associatively derived. There are, therefore, certain external methods, which every teacher knows, of voluntarily arousing the attention from time to time and keeping it upon the subject. Mr. Fitch has a lecture on the art of securing attention, and he briefly passes these methods in review; the posture must be changed; places can be changed. Questions, after being answered singly, may occasionally be answered in concert. Elliptical questions may be asked, the pupil supplying the missing word. The teacher must pounce upon the most listless child and wake him up. The habit of prompt and ready response must be kept up. Recapitulations, illustrations, examples, novelty of order, and ruptures of routine,—all these are means for keeping the attention alive and contributing a little interest to a dull subject. Above all, the teacher must himself be alive and ready, and must use the contagion of his own example.

But, when all is said and done, the fact remains that

some teachers have a naturally inspiring presence, and can make their exercises interesting, while others simply cannot. And psychology and general pedagogy here confess their failure, and hand things over to the deeper springs of human personality to conduct the task.

A brief reference to the physiological theory of the attentive process may serve still further to elucidate these practical remarks, and confirm them by showing them from a slightly different point of view.

What is the attentive process, psychologically considered? Attention to an object is what takes place whenever that object most completely occupies the mind. For simplicity's sake suppose the object be an object of sensation, —a figure approaching us at a distance on the road. It is far off, barely perceptible, and hardly moving: we do not know with certainty whether it is a man or not. Such an object as this, if carelessly looked at, may hardly catch our attention at all. The optical impression may affect solely the marginal consciousness, while the mental focus keeps engaged with rival things. We may indeed not 'see' it till some one points it out. But, if so, how does he point it out? By his finger, and by describing its appearance,—by creating a premonitory image of *where* to look and of *what* to expect to see. This premonitory image is already an excitement of the same nerve-centres that are to be concerned with the impression. The impression comes, and excites them still further; and now the object enters the focus of the field, consciousness being sustained both by impression and by preliminary idea. But the maximum of attention to it is not yet reached. Although we see it, we may not care for it; it may suggest nothing important to us; and a rival stream of objects or of thoughts may quickly take our mind away. If, however, our companion defines it in a significant way, arouses in the mind a set of experiences to be apprehended from it,—names it an enemy or as a messenger of important tidings,—the residual and marginal ideas now aroused, so far from being its rivals, become its associates and allies. They shoot together into one system with it; they converge upon it; they keep it steadily in focus; the mind attends to it with maximum power.

The attentive process, therefore, at its maximum may be physiologically symbolized by a brain-cell played on in two ways, from without and from within. Incoming currents from the periphery arouse it, and collateral currents from the centres of memory and imagination re-enforce these.

In this process the incoming impression is the newer element; the ideas which re-enforce and sustain it are among the older possessions of the mind. And the maximum of attention may then be said to be found whenever we have a systematic harmony or unification between the novel and the old. It is an odd circumstance that neither the old nor the new, by itself, is interesting; the absolutely old is insipid; the absolutely new makes no appeal at all. The old *in* the new is what claims the attention,—the old with a slightly new turn. No one wants to hear a lecture on a subject completely disconnected with his previous knowledge, but we all like lectures on subjects of which we know a little already, just as, in the fashions, every year must bring its slight modification of last year's suit, but an abrupt jump from the fashion of one decade into another would be distasteful to the eye.

The genius of the interesting teacher consists in sympathetic divination of the sort of material with which the pupil's mind is likely to be already spontaneously engaged, and in the ingenuity which discovers paths of connection from that material to the matters to be newly learned. The principle is easy to grasp, but the accomplishment is difficult in the extreme. And a knowledge of such psychology as this which I am recalling can no more make a good teacher than a knowledge of the laws of perspective can make a landscape painter of effective skill.

A certain doubt may now occur to some of you. A while ago, apropos of the pugnacious instinct, I spoke of our modern pedagogy as being possibly too 'soft.' You may perhaps here face me with my own words, and ask whether the exclusive effort on the teacher's part to keep the pupil's spontaneous interest going, and to avoid the more strenuous path of voluntary attention to repulsive work, does not savor also of sentimentalism. The greater part of schoolroom work, you say, must, in the nature of things, always be repulsive. To face uninteresting drudgery is a good part of life's work. Why seek to eliminate it from the schoolroom or minimize the sterner law?

A word or two will obviate what might perhaps become a serious misunderstanding here.

It is certain that most schoolroom work, till it has become habitual and automatic, is repulsive, and cannot be done without voluntarily jerking back the attention to it every now and then. This is inevitable, let the teacher do what he will. It flows from the inherent nature of the subjects and of the learning mind. The repulsive processes of verbal memorizing, of discovering steps of mathematical identity, and the like, must borrow their interest at first from purely external sources, mainly from the personal interests with which success in mastering them is associated, such as gaining of rank, avoiding punishment, not being beaten by a difficulty and the like. Without such borrowed interest, the child could not attend to them at all. But in these processes what becomes interesting enough to be attended to is not thereby attended to *without effort*. Effort always has to go on, derived interest, for the most part, not awakening attention that is *easy*, however spontaneous it may now have to be called. The interest which the teacher, by his utmost skill, can lend to the subject, proves over and over again to be only an interest sufficient *to let loose the effort*. The teacher, therefore, need never concern himself about *inventing* occasions where effort must be called into play. Let him still awaken whatever sources of interest in the subject he can by stirring up connections between it and the pupil's nature, whether in the line of theoretic curiosity, of personal interest, or of pugnacious impulse. The laws of mind will then bring enough pulses of effort into play to keep the pupil exercised in the direction of the subject. There is, in fact, no greater school of effort than the steady struggle to attend to immediately repulsive or difficult objects of thought which have grown to interest us through their association as means, with some remote ideal end.

The Herbartian doctrine of interest ought not, therefore, in principle to be reproached with making pedagogy soft. If it do so, it is because it is unintelligently carried on. Do not, then, for the mere sake of discipline, command attention from your pupils in thundering tones. Do not too often beg it from them as a favor, nor claim it as a right, nor try habitually to excite it by preaching the importance of the subject. Sometimes, indeed, you must do these things; but, the more you have to do them, the less skilful teacher you will show yourself to be. Elicit interest from within, by the warmth with which you care for the topic yourself, and by following the laws I have laid down.

If the topic be highly abstract, show its nature by concrete examples. If it be unfamiliar, trace some point of analogy in it with the known. If it be inhuman, make it figure as part of a story. If it be difficult, couple its acquisition with some prospect of personal gain. Above all things, make sure that it shall run through certain inner changes, since no unvarying object can possibly hold the mental field for long. Let your pupil wander from one aspect to another of your subject, if you do not wish him to wander from it altogether to something else, variety in unity being the secret of all interesting talk and thought. The relation of all these things to the native genius of the instructor is too obvious to need comment again.

One more point, and I am done with the subject of attention. There is unquestionably a great native variety among individuals in the type of their attention. Some of us are naturally scatter-brained, and others follow easily a train of connected thoughts without temptation to swerve aside to other subjects. This seems to depend on a difference between individuals in the type of their field of consciousness. In some persons this is highly focalized and concentrated, and the focal ideas predominate in determining association. In others we must suppose the margin to be brighter, and to be filled with something like meteoric showers of images, which strike into it at random, displacing the focal ideas, and carrying association in their own direction. Persons of the latter type find their attention wandering every minute, and must bring it back by a voluntary pull. The others sink into a subject of meditation deeply, and, when interrupted, are 'lost' for a moment before they come back to the outer world.

The possession of such a steady faculty of attention is unquestionably a great boon. Those who have it can work more rapidly, and with less nervous wear and tear. I am inclined to think that no one who is without it naturally can by any amount of drill or discipline attain it in a very high degree. Its amount is probably a fixed characteristic of the individual. But I wish to make a remark here which I shall have occasion to make again in other connections. It is that no one need deplore unduly the inferiority in himself of any one elementary faculty. This concentrated type of attention is an elementary faculty: it is one of the things that might be ascertained and measured by exercises in the laboratory. But, having ascertained it in a number of persons, we could never rank them in a scale of actual and practical mental efficiency based on its degrees. The total mental efficiency of a man is the resultant of the working together of all his faculties. He is too complex a being for any one of them to have the casting vote. If any one of them do have the casting vote, it is more likely to be the strength of his desire and passion, the strength of the interest he takes in what is proposed. Concentration, memory, reasoning power, inventiveness, excellence of the senses,—all are subsidiary to this. No matter how scatter-brained the type of a man's successive fields of consciousness may be, if he really *care* for a subject, he will return to it incessantly from his incessant wanderings, and first and last do more with it, and get more results from it, than another person whose attention may be more continuous during a given interval, but whose passion for the subject is of a more languid and less permanent sort. Some of the most efficient workers I know are of the ultra-scatter-brained type. One friend, who does a prodigious quantity of work, has in fact confessed to me that, if he wants to get ideas on any subject, he sits down to work at something else, his best results coming through his mind-wanderings. This is perhaps an epigrammatic exaggeration on his part; but I seriously think that no one of us need be too much distressed at his own shortcomings in this regard. Our mind may enjoy but little comfort, may be restless and feel confused; but it may be extremely efficient all the same.

CHAPTER 12

Memory

WE ARE following a somewhat arbitrary order. Since each and every faculty we possess is either in whole or in part a resultant of the play of our associations, it would have been as natural, after treating of association, to treat of memory as to treat of interest and attention next. But, since we did take the latter operations first, we must take memory now without farther delay; for the phenomena of memory are among the simplest and most immediate consequences of the fact that our mind is essentially an associating machine. There is no more pre-eminent example for exhibiting the fertility of the laws of association as principles of psychological analysis. Memory, moreover, is so important a faculty in the schoolroom that you are probably waiting with some eagerness to know what psychology has to say about it for your help.

In old times, if you asked a person to explain why he

came to be remembering at that moment some particular incident in his previous life, the only reply he could make was that his soul is endowed with a faculty called memory; that it is the inalienable function of this faculty to recollect; and that, therefore, he necessarily at that moment must have a cognition of that portion of the past. This explanation by a 'faculty' is one thing which explanation by association has superseded altogether. If, by saying we have a faculty of memory, you mean nothing more than the fact that we can remember, nothing more than an abstract name for our power inwardly to recall the past, there is no harm done: we do have the faculty; for we unquestionably have such a power. But if, by faculty, you mean a principle of *explanation of our general power to recall,* your psychology is empty. The associationist psychology, on the other hand, gives an explanation of each particular fact of recollection; and, in so doing, it also gives an explanation of the general faculty. The 'faculty' of memory is thus no real or ultimate explanation; for it is itself explained as a result of the association of ideas.

Nothing is easier than to show you just what I mean by this. Suppose I am silent for a moment, and then say in commanding accents: "Remember! Recollect!" Does your faculty of memory obey the order, and reproduce any definite image for your past? Certainly not. It stands staring into vacancy, and asking, "What kind of a thing do you wish me to remember?" It needs in short, a *cue.* But, if I say, remember the date of your birth, or remember what you had for breakfast, or remember the succession of notes in the musical scale; then your faculty of memory immediately produces the required result: the 'cue' determines its vast set of potentialities toward a particular point. And if you now look to see how this happens, you immediately perceive that the cue is something *contiguously associated* with the thing recalled. The words, 'date of my birth,' have an ingrained association with a particular number, month, and year; the words, 'breakfast this morning,' cut off all other lines of recall except those which lead to coffee and bacon and eggs; the words, 'musical scale,' are inveterate mental neighbors of do, ré, mi, fa, sol, la, etc. The laws of association govern, in fact, all the trains of our thinking which are not interrupted by sensations breaking on us from without. Whatever appears in the mind must be *introduced*; and, when introduced, it is as the associate of something already there. This is as true of what you are recollecting as it is of everything else you think of.

Reflection will show you that there are peculiarities in your memory which would be quite whimsical and unaccountable if we were forced to regard them as the product of a purely spiritual faculty. Were memory such a faculty, granted to us solely for its practical use, we ought to remember easiest whatever we most *needed* to remember; and frequency of repetition, recency, and the like, would play no part in the matter. That we should best remember frequent things and recent things, and forget things that are ancient or were experienced only once, could only be regarded as an incomprehensible anomaly on such a view. But if we remember because of our associations, and if these are (as the physiological psychologists believe) due to our organized brain-paths, we easily see how the law of recency and repetition should prevail. Paths frequently and recently ploughed are those that lie most open, those which may be expected most easily to lead to results. The laws of our memory, as we find them, therefore are incidents of our associational constitution; and, when we are emancipated from the flesh, it is conceivable that they may no longer continue to obtain.

We may assume, then, that recollection is a resultant of our associative processes, these themselves in the last analysis being most probably due to the workings of our brain.

Descending more particularly into the faculty of memory, we have to distinguish between its potential aspect as a magazine or storehouse and its actual aspect as recollection now of a particular event. Our memory contains all sorts of items which we do not now recall, but which we may recall, provided a sufficient cue be offered. Both the general retention and the special recall are explained by association. An educated memory depends on an organized system of associations; and its goodness depends on two of their peculiarities: first, on the persistency of the associations; and, second, on their number.

Let us consider each of these points in turn.

First, the persistency of the associations. This gives what may be called the *quality of native retentiveness* to the individual. If, as I think we are forced to, we consider the brain to be the organic condition by which the vestiges of our experience are associated with each other, we may suppose that some brains are 'wax to receive and marble to retain.' The slightest impressions made on them abide. Names, dates, prices, anecdotes, quotations, are indelibly retained, their several elements fixedly cohering together, so that the individual soon becomes a walking cyclopædia of information. All this may occur with no philosophic tendency in the mind, no impulse to weave the materials acquired into anything like a logical system. In the books of anecdotes, and, more recently, in the psychology-books, we find recorded instances of monstrosities, as we may call them, of this desultory memory; and they are often otherwise very stupid men. It is, of course, by no means incompatible with a philosophic mind; for mental characteristics have infinite capacities for permutation. And, when both memory and philosophy combine together in one person, then indeed we have the highest sort of intellectual efficiency. Your Walter Scotts, your Leibnitzes, your Gladstones, and your Goethes, all your folio copies of mankind, belong to this type. Efficiency on a colossal scale would indeed seem to require it. For, although your philosophic or systematic mind without good desultory memory may know how to work out results and recollect where in the books to find them, the time lost in the searching process handicaps the thinker, and gives to the more ready type of individual the economical advantage.

The extreme of the contrasted type, the type with associations of small persistency, is found in those who have almost no desultory memory at all. If they are also deficient in logical and systematizing power, we call them simply feeble intellects; and no more need to be said about them here. Their brain-matter, we may imagine, is like a fluid jelly, in which impressions may be easily made, but are soon closed over again, so that the brain reverts to its original indifferent state.

But it may occur here, just as in other gelatinous substances, that an impression will vibrate throughout the brain, and send waves into other parts of it. In cases of this sort, although the immediate impression may fade out quickly, it does modify the cerebral mass; for the paths it makes there may remain, and become so many avenues through which the impression may be reproduced if they ever get excited again. And its liability to reproduction will depend of course upon the variety of these paths and upon the frequency with which they are used. Each path is in fact an associated process, the number of these associates becoming thus to a great degree a substitute for the independent tenacity of the original impression. As I have elsewhere written: Each of the associates is a hook to which it hangs, a means to fish it up when sunk below the surface. Together they form a network of attachments by which it is woven into the entire tissue of our thought. The 'secret of a good memory' is thus the secret of forming diverse and multiple associations with every fact we care to retain. But this forming of associations with a fact,—what is it but thinking *about* the fact as much as possible? Briefly, then, of two men with the same outward experiences, *the one who thinks over his experiences most*, and weaves them into the most systematic relations with each other, will be the one with the best memory.

But, if our ability to recollect a thing be so largely a matter of its associations with other things which thus becomes its cues, an important pædagogic consequence follows. *There can be no improvement of the general or elementary faculty of memory: there can only be improvement of our memory for special systems of associated things*; and this latter improvement is due to the way in which the things in question are woven into association with each other in the mind. Intricately or profoundly woven, they are held: disconnected, they tend to drop out just in proportion as the native brain retentiveness is poor. And no amount of training, drilling, repeating, and reciting employed upon the matter of one system of objects, the history-system, for example, will in the least improve either the facility or the durability with which objects belonging to a wholly disparate system—the system of facts of chemistry, for instance—tend to be retained. That system must be separately worked into the mind by itself,—a chemical fact which is thought about in connection with the other chemical facts, tending then to stay, but otherwise easily dropping out.

We have, then, not so much a faculty of memory as many faculties of memory. We have as many as we have systems of objects habitually thought of in connection with each other. A given object is held in the memory by the associates it has acquired within its own system exclusively. Learning the facts of another system will in no wise help it to stay in the mind, for the simple reason that it has no 'cues' within that other system.

We see examples of this on every hand. Most men have a good memory for facts connected with their own pursuits. A college athlete, who remains a dunce at his books, may amaze you by his knowledge of the 'records' at various feats and games, and prove himself a walking dictionary of sporting statistics. The reason is that he is constantly going over these things in his mind, and comparing and making series of them. They form for him, not so many odd facts, but a concept-system, so they stick. So the merchant remembers prices, the politician other politician's speeches and votes, with a copiousness which astonishes outsiders, but which the amount of thinking they bestow on these subjects easily explains.

The great memory for facts which a Darwin or a Spencer reveal in their books is not incompatible with the possession on their part of a mind with only a middling degree of physiological retentiveness. Let a man early in life set himself the task of verifying such a theory as that of evolution, and facts will soon cluster and cling to him like grapes to their stem. Their relations to the theory will hold them fast; and, the more of these the mind is able to discern, the greater the erudition will become. Meanwhile the theorist may have little, if any, desultory memory. Unutilizable facts may be unnoted by him, and forgotten as soon as heard. An ignorance almost as encyclopedic as his erudition may coexist with the latter, and hide, as it were, within the interstices of its web. Those of you who have had much to do with scholars and *savants* will readily think of examples of the class of mind I mean.

The best possible sort of system into which to weave an object, mentally, is a *rational* system, or what is called a 'science.' Place the thing in its pigeon-hole in a classificatory series; explain it logically by its causes, and deduce from it its necessary effects; find out of what natural law it is an instance,—and you then know it in the best of all possible ways. A 'science' is thus the greatest of labor-saving contrivances. It relieves the memory of an immense number of details, replacing, as it does, merely contiguous associations by the logical ones of identity, similarity, or analogy. If you know a 'law,' you may discharge your memory of masses of particular instances, for the law will reproduce them for you whenever you require them. The law of refraction, for example: If you know that, you can with a pencil and a bit of paper immediately discern how a convex lens, a concave lens, or a prism, must severally alter the appearance of an object. But, if you don't know the general law, you must charge your memory separately with each of the three kinds of effect.

A 'philosophic' system, in which all things found their rational explanation and were connected together as causes and effects, would be the perfect mnemonic system, in which the greatest economy of means would bring about the greatest richness of results. So that, if we have poor desultory memories, we can save ourselves by cultivating the philosophic turn of mind.

There are many artificial systems of mnemonics, some public, some sold as secrets. They are all so many devices for training us into certain methodical and stereotyped *ways of thinking* about the facts we seek to retain. Even were I competent, I could not here go into these systems in any detail. But a single example, from a popular system, will show what I mean. I take the number-alphabet, the great mnemonic device for recollecting numbers and dates. In this system each digit is represented by a consonant, thus: 1 is *t* or *d*; 2, *n*; 3, *m*; 4, *r*; 5, *l*; 6, *sh*, *j*, *ch*, or *g*; 7, *c*, *k*, *g*, or *qu*; 8, *f* or *v*; 9, *b* or *p*; 0, *s*, *c*, or *z*. Suppose, now, you wish to remember the velocity of sound, 1,142 feet a second: *t*, *t*, *r*, *n*, are the letters you must use. They make the consonants of *tight run*, and it would be a 'tight run' for you to keep up such a speed. So 1649, the date of the execution of Charles I., may be remembered by the word *sharp*, which recalls the headsman's axe.

Apart from the extreme difficulty of finding words that are appropriate in this exercise, it is clearly an excessively poor, trivial, and silly way of 'thinking' about dates; and the way of the historian is much better. He has a lot of land-mark-dates already in his mind. He knows the historic concatenation of events, and can usually place an event at its right date in the chronology-table, by thinking of it in a rational way, referring it to its antecedents, tracing its concomitants and consequences, and thus ciphering out its date by connecting it with theirs. The artificial memory-systems, recommending, as they do, such irrational methods of thinking, are only to be recommended for the first land-marks in a system, or for such purely detached facts as enjoy no rational connection with the rest of our ideas. Thus the student of physics may remember the order of the spectral colours by the word *vibgyor* which their initial letters make. The student of anatomy may remember the position of the Mitral valve on the Left side of the heart by thinking that L. M. stands also for 'long meter' in the hymn-books.

You now see why 'cramming' must be so poor a mode of study. Cramming seeks to stamp things in by intense application immediately before the ordeal. But a thing thus learned can form but few associations. On the other hand, the same thing recurring on different days, in different contexts, read, recited on, referred to again and again, related to other things and reviewed, gets well wrought into the mental structure. This is the reason why you should enforce on your pupils habits of continuous application. There is no moral turpitude in cramming. It would be the best, because the most economical, mode of study if it led to the results desired. But it does not, and your older pupils can readily be made to see the reason why.

It follows also, from what has been said, that *the popular idea that 'the Memory,' in the sense of a general elementary faculty, can be improved by training, is a great mistake.* Your memory for facts of a certain class can be improved very much by training in that class of facts, because the incoming new fact will then find all sorts of analogues and associates already there, and these will keep it liable to recall. But other kinds of fact will reap none of that benefit, and, unless one have been also trained and versed in *their* class, will be at the mercy of the mere crude retentiveness of the individual, which, as we have seen, is practically a fixed quantity. Nevertheless, one often hears people say: "A great sin was committed against me in my youth: my teachers entirely failed to exercise my memory. If they had only made me learn a lot of things by heart at school, I should not be, as I am now, forgetful of everything I read and hear." This is a great mistake: learning poetry by heart will make it easier to learn and remember other poetry, but nothing else; and so of dates; and so of chemistry and geography.

But, after what I have said, I am sure you will need no farther argument on this point; and I therefore pass it by.

But, since it has brought me to speak of learning things by heart, I think that a general practical remark about verbal memorizing may now not be out of place. The excesses of old-fashioned verbal memorizing, and the immense advantages of object-teaching in the earlier stages of culture, have perhaps led those who philosophize about teaching to an unduly strong reaction; and learning things by heart is now probably somewhat too much despised.

For, when all is said and done, the fact remains that verbal material is, on the whole, the handiest and most useful material in which thinking can be carried on. Abstract conceptions are far and away the most economical instruments of thought, and abstract conceptions are fixed and incarnated for us in words. Statistical inquiry would seem to show that, as men advance in life, they tend to make less and less use of visual images, and more and more use of words. One of the first things that Mr. Galton discovered was that this appeared to be the case with the members of the Royal Society whom he questioned as to their mental images. I should say, therefore, that constant exercise in verbal memorizing must still be an indispensable feature in all sound education. Nothing is more deplorable than that inarticulate and helpless sort of mind that is reminded by everything of some quotation, case, or anecdote, which it cannot now exactly recollect. Nothing, on the other hand, is more convenient to its possessor, or more delightful to his comrades, than a mind able, in telling a story, to give the exact words of the dialogue or to furnish a quotation accurate and complete. In every branch of study there are happily turned, concise, and handy formulas which in an incomparable way sum up results. The mind that can retain such formulas is in so far a superior mind, and the communication of them to the pupil ought always to be one of the teacher's favorite tasks.

In learning 'by heart,' there are, however, efficient and inefficient methods; and, by making the pupil skilful in the best method, the teacher can both interest him and abridge the task. The best method is of course not to 'hammer in' the sentences, by mere reiteration, but to analyze them, and think. For example, if the pupil should have to learn this last sentence, let him first strip out its grammatical core, and learn, "The best method is not to hammer in, but to analyze," and then add the amplificative and restrictive clauses, bit by bit, thus: "The best method is of course not to hammer in *the sentences,* but to analyze *them and think.*" Then finally insert the words '*by mere reiteration,*' and the sentence is complete, and both better understood

and quicker remembered than by a more purely mechani
cal method.

In conclusion, I must say a word about the contributions
to our knowledge of memory which have recently come
from the laboratory-psychologists. Many of the enthusiasts
for scientific or brass-instrument child-study are taking accurate measurements of children's elementary faculties, and
among these what we may call *immediate memory* admits
of easy measurement. All we need do is to exhibit to the
child a series of letters, syllables, figures, pictures, or what-
not, at intervals of one, two, three, or more seconds, or to
sound a similar series of names at the same intervals, within
his hearing, and then see how completely he can reproduce
the list, either directly, or after an interval of ten, twenty,
or sixty seconds, or some longer space of time. According to
the results of this exercise, the pupils may be rated in a
memory-scale; and some persons go so far as to think that
the teacher should modify her treatment of the child according to the strength or feebleness of its faculty as thus
made known.

Now I can only repeat here what I said to you when
treating of attention: man is too complex a being for light
to be thrown on his real efficiency by measuring any one
mental faculty taken apart from its consensus in the working whole. Such an exercise as this, dealing with incoherent
and insipid objects, with no logical connection with each
other, or practical significance outside of the 'test,' is an
exercise the like of which in real life we are hardly ever
called upon to perform. In real life, our memory is always
used in the service of some interest: we remember things
which we care for or which are associated with things we
care for; and the child who stands at the bottom of the
scale thus experimentally established might, by dint of the
strength of his passion for a subject, and in consequence of
the logical association into which he weaves the actual materials of his experience, be a very effective memorizer
indeed, and do his school-tasks on the whole much better

than an immediate parrot who might stand at the top of the 'scientifically accurate' list.

This preponderance of interest, of passion, in determining the results of a human being's working life, obtains throughout. No elementary measurement, capable of being performed in a laboratory, can throw any light on the actual efficiency of the subject; for the vital thing about him, his emotional and moral energy and doggedness, can be measured by no single experiment, and becomes known only by the total results in the long run. A blind man like Huber, with his passion for bees and ants, can observe them through other people's eyes better than these can through their own. A man born with neither arms nor legs, like the late Kavanagh, M. P.—and what an icy heart his mother must have had about him in his babyhood, and how 'negative' would the laboratory-measurements of his motor-functions have been!—can be an adventurous traveller, an equestrian and sportsman, and lead an athletic outdoor life. Mr. Romanes studied the elementary rate of apperception in a large number of persons by making them read a paragraph as fast as they could take it in, and then immediately write down all they could reproduce of its contents. He found astonishing differences in the rapidity, some taking four times as long as others to absorb the paragraph, and the swiftest readers being, as a rule, the best immediate recollectors, too. But not,—and this is my point, —*not* the most *intellectually capable subjects,* as tested by the results of what Mr. Romanes rightly names 'genuine' intellectual work; for he tried the experiment with several highly distinguished men in science and literature, and most of them turned out to be slow readers.

In the light of all such facts one may well believe that the total impression which a perceptive teacher will get of the pupil's condition, as indicated by his general temper and manner, by the listlessness or alertness, by the ease or painfulness with which his school work is done, will be of much more value than those unreal experimental tests, those pedantic elementary measurements of fatigue, memory, association, and attention, etc., which are urged upon us as the only basis of a genuinely scientific pedagogy. Such measurements can give us useful information only when we combine them with observations made without brass instruments, upon the total demeanor of the measured individual, by teachers with eyes in their heads and common sense, and some feeling for the concrete facts of human nature in their hearts.

Depend upon it, no one need be too much cast down by the discovery of his deficiency in any elementary faculty of the mind. What tells in life is the whole mind working together, and the deficiencies of any one faculty can be compensated by the efforts of the rest. You can be an artist without visual images, a reader without eyes, a mass of erudition with a bad elementary memory. In almost any subject your passion for the subject will save you. If you only care enough for a result, you will almost certainly attain it. If you wish to be rich, you will be rich; if you wish to be learned, you will be learned; if you wish to be good, you will be good. Only you must, then, *really* wish these things, and wish them with exclusiveness, and not wish at the same time a hundred other incompatible things just as strongly.

One of the most important discoveries of the 'scientific' sort that have recently been made in psychology is that of Mr. Galton and others concerning the great variations among individuals in the type of their imagination. Every one is now familiar with the fact that human beings vary enormously in the brilliancy, completeness, definiteness, and extent of their visual images. These are singularly perfect in a large number of individuals, and in a few are so rudimentary as hardly to exist. The same is true of the auditory and motor images, and probably of those of every kind; and the recent discovery of distinct brain-areas for the various orders of sensation would seem to provide a physical basis for such variations and discrepancies. The facts, as I said, are nowadays so popularly known that I need only remind you of their existence. They might seem at first sight of practical importance to the teacher; and, indeed, teachers have been recommended to sort their pupils in this way, and treat them as the result falls out. You should interrogate them as to their imagery, it is said, or exhibit lists of written words to their eyes, and then sound similar lists in their ears, and see by which channel a child retains most words. Then, in dealing with that child, make your appeals predominantly through that channel. If the class were very small, results of some distinctness might doubtless thus be obtained by a painstaking teacher. But it is obvious that in the usual school-room no such differentiation of appeal is possible; and the only really useful practical lesson that emerges from this analytic psychology in the conduct of large schools is the lesson already reached in a purely empirical way, that the teacher ought always to impress the class through as many sensible channels as he can. Talk and write and draw on blackboard, permit the pupils to talk, and make them write and draw, exhibit pictures, plans, and curves, have your diagrams colored differently in the different parts, etc.; and out of the whole variety of impressions the individual child will find the most lasting ones for himself. In all primary school work this principle of multiple impressions is well recognized, so I need say no more about it here.

This principle of multiplying channels and varying associations and appeals is important, not only for teaching pupils to remember, but for teaching them to understand. It runs, in fact, through the whole teaching art.

One word about the unconscious and unreproducible part of our acquisitions, and I shall have done with the topic of memory.

Professor Ebbinghaus, in a heroic little investigation into the laws of memory which he performed a dozen or more years ago by the method of learning lists of nonsense syllables, devised a method of measuring the rate of our forgetfulness, which lays bare an important law of the mind.

His method was to read over his list until he could repeat it once by heart unhesitatingly. The number of repetitions required for this was a measure of the difficulty of the learning in each particular case. Now, after having once learned a piece in this way, if we wait five minutes, we find it impossible to repeat it again in the same unhesitating manner. We must read it over again to revive some of the syllables, which have already dropped out or got transposed. Ebbinghaus now systematically studied the number of readings-over which were necessary to revive the unhesitating recollection of the piece after five minutes, half an hour, an hour, a day, a week, a month, had elapsed. The number of rereadings required he took to be a measure of the *amount of forgetting* that had occurred in the elapsed interval. And he found some remarkable facts. The process of forgetting, namely, is vastly more rapid at first than later on. Thus full half of the piece seems to be forgotten within the first half-hour, two-thirds of it are forgotten at the end of eight hours, but only four-fifths at the end of a month. He made no trials beyond one month of interval; but, if we ourselves prolong ideally the curve of remembrance, whose beginning his experiments thus obtain, it is natural to suppose that, no matter how long a time might elapse, the curve would never descend quite so low as to touch the zero-line. In other words, no matter how long ago we may have learned a poem, and no matter how complete our inability to reproduce it now may be, yet the first learning will still show its lingering effects in the abridgment of the time required for learning it again. In short, Professor Ebbinghaus's experiments show that things which we are quite unable definitely to recall have nevertheless impressed themselves, in some way, upon the structure of the mind. We are different for having once learned them. The resistances in our systems of brain-paths are altered. Our apprehensions are quickened. Our conclusions from certain premises are probably not just what they would be if those modifications were not there. The latter influence the whole margin of our consciousness, even though their products, not being distinctly reproducible, do not directly figure at the focus of the field.

The teacher should draw a lesson from these facts. We are all too apt to measure the gains of our pupils by their

proficiency in directly reproducing in a recitation or an examination such matters as they may have learned, and inarticulate power in them is something of which we always
underestimate the value. The boy who tells us, "I know the
answer, but I can't say what it is," we treat as practically
identical with him who knows absolutely nothing about
the answer at all. But this is a great mistake. It is but a
small part of our experience in life that we are ever able
articulately to recall. And yet the whole of it has had its influence in shaping our character and defining our tendencies to judge and act. Although the ready memory is a great
blessing to its possessor, the vaguer memory of a subject, of
having once had to do with it, of its neighborhood, and of
where we may go to recover it again, constitutes in most
men and women the chief fruit of their education. This is
true even in professional education. The doctor, the lawyer,
are seldom able to decide upon a case off-hand. They differ
from other men only through the fact that they know how
to get at the materials for decision in five minutes or half
an hour: whereas the layman is unable to get at the materials at all, not knowing in what books and indexes to
look or not understanding the technical terms.

Be patient, then, and sympathetic with the type of mind
that cuts a poor figure in examinations. It may, in the long
examination which life sets us, come out in the end in better shape than the glib and ready reproducer, its passions
being deeper, its purposes more worthy, its combining
power less commonplace, and its total mental output consequently more important.

Such are the chief points which it has seemed worth
while for me to call to your notice under the head of memory. We can sum them up for practical purposes by saying
that the art of remembering is the art of *thinking*; and by
adding, with Dr. Pick, that, when we wish to fix a new
thing in either our own mind or a pupil's, our conscious
effort should not be so much to *impress* and *retain* it as to
connect it with something else already there. The connecting *is* the thinking; and, if we attend clearly to the connec-

tion, the connected thing will certainly be likely to remain within recall.

I shall next ask you to consider the process by which we acquire new knowledge,—the process of 'Apperception,' as it is called, by which we receive and deal with new experiences, and revise our stock of ideas so as to form new or improved conceptions.

CHAPTER 13

The Acquisition of Ideas

THE IMAGES of our past experiences, of whatever nature they may be, visual or verbal, blurred and dim, vivid and distinct, abstract or concrete, need not be memory images, in the strict sense of the word. That is, they need not rise before the mind in a marginal fringe or context of concomitant circumstances, which mean for us their *date*. They may be mere conceptions, floating pictures of an object, or of its type or class. In this undated condition, we call them products of 'imagination' or 'conception.' Imagination is the term commonly used where the object represented is thought of as an individual thing. Conception is the term where we think of it as a type or class. For our present purpose the distinction is not important; and I will permit myself to use either the word 'conception,' or the still vaguer word 'idea,' to designate the inner objects of contemplation, whether these be individual things, like 'the sun' or 'Julius Cæsar,' or classes of things, like 'animal kingdom,' or, finally, entirely abstract attributes, like 'rationality' or 'rectitude.'

The result of our education is to fill the mind little by

little, as experiences accrete, with a stock of such ideas. In the illustration I used at our first meeting, of the child snatching the toy and getting slapped, the vestiges left by the first experience answered to so many ideas which he acquired thereby,—ideas that remained with him associated in a certain order, and from the last one of which the child eventually proceeded to act. The sciences of grammar and of logic are little more than attempts methodically to classify all such acquired ideas and to trace certain laws of relationship among them. The forms of relation between them, becoming themselves in turn noticed by the mind, are treated as conceptions of a higher and more abstract order, as when we speak of a 'syllogistic relation' between propositions, or of four quantities making a 'proportion,' or of the 'inconsistency' of two conceptions, or the 'implication' of one in the other.

So you see that the process of education, taken in a large way, may be described as nothing but the process of acquiring ideas or conceptions, the best educated mind being the mind which has the largest stock of them, ready to meet the largest possible variety of the emergencies of life. The lack of education means only the failure to have acquired them, and the consequent liability to be 'floored' and 'rattled' in the vicissitudes of experience.

In all this process of acquiring conceptions, a certain instinctive order is followed. There is a native tendency to assimilate certain kinds of conception at one age, and other kinds of conception at a later age. During the first seven or eight years of childhood the mind is most interested in the sensible properties of material things. *Constructiveness* is the instinct most active; and by the incessant hammering and sawing, and dressing and undressing dolls, putting of things together and taking them apart, the child not only trains the muscles to co-ordinate action, but accumulates a store of physical conceptions which are the basis of his knowledge of the material world through life. Object-teaching and manual training wisely extend the sphere of this order of acquisition. Clay, wood, metals, and the various kinds of tools are made to contribute to the store. A youth brought up with a sufficiently broad basis of this kind is always at home in the world. He stands within the pale. He is acquainted with Nature, and Nature in a certain sense is acquainted with him. Whereas the youth brought up alone at home, with no acquaintance with anything but the printed page, is always afflicted with a certain remoteness from the material facts of life, and a correlative insecurity of consciousness which make of him a kind of alien on the earth in which he ought to feel himself perfectly at home.

I already said something of this in speaking of the constructive impulse, and I must not repeat myself. Moreover, you fully realize, I am sure, how important for life,— for the moral tone of life, quite apart from definite practical pursuits,—is this sense of readiness for emergencies which a man gains through early familiarity and acquaintance with the world of material things. To have grown up on a farm, to have haunted a carpenter's and blacksmith's shop, to have handled horses and cows and boats and guns, and to have ideas and abilities connected with such objects are an inestimable part of youthful acquisition. After adolescence it is rare to be able to get into familiar touch with any of these primitive things. The instinctive propensions have faded, and the habits are hard to acquire.

Accordingly, one of the best fruits of the 'child-study' movement has been to reinstate all these activities to their proper place in a sound system of education. *Feed* the growing human being, feed him with the sort of experience for which from year to year he shows a natural craving, and he will develop in adult life a sounder sort of mental tissue, even though he may seem to be 'wasting' a great deal of his growing time, in the eyes of those for whom the only channels of learning are books and verbally communicated information.

It is not till adolescence is reached that the mind grows able to take in the more abstract aspects of experience, the hidden similarities and distinctions between things, and especially their causal sequences. Rational knowledge of such things as mathematics, mechanics, chemistry, and biology, is now possible; and the acquisition of conceptions of this order form the next phase of education. Later still, not till adolescence is well advanced, does the mind awaken to a systematic interest in abstract human relations —moral relations, properly so called,—to sociological ideas and to metaphysical abstractions.

This general order of sequence is followed traditionally of course in the schoolroom. It is foreign to my purpose to do more than indicate that general psychological principle of the successive order of awakening of the faculties on which the whole thing rests. I have spoken of it already, apropos of the transitoriness of instincts. Just as many a youth has to go permanently without an adequate stock of conceptions of a certain order, because experiences of that order were not yielded at the time when new curiosity was most acute, so it will conversely happen that many another youth is spoiled for a certain subject of study (although he would have enjoyed it well if led into it at a later age) through having had it thrust upon him so prematurely that disgust was created, and the bloom quite taken off from future trials. I think I have seen college students unfitted forever for 'philosophy' from having taken that study up a year too soon.

In all these later studies, verbal material is the vehicle by which the mind thinks. The abstract conceptions of physics and sociology may, it is true, be embodied in visual or other images of phenomena, but they need not be so; and the truth remains that, after adolescence has begun, "words, words, words," must constitute a large part, and an always larger part as life advances, of what the human being has to learn. This is so even in the natural sciences, so far as these are causal and rational, and not merely confined to description. So I go back to what I said awhile ago apropos of verbal memorizing. The more accurately words are learned, the better, if only the teacher make sure that what they signify is also understood. It is the failure of this latter condition, in so much of the old-fashioned recitation, that has caused that reaction against 'parrot-like reproduction' that we are so familiar with today. A friend of mine, visiting a school, was asked to examine a young class in geography. Glancing at the book, she said: "Suppose you should dig a hole in the ground, hundreds of feet deep, how should you find it at the bottom,—warmer or colder than on top?" None of the class replying, the teacher said: "I'm sure they know, but I think you don't ask the question quite rightly. Let me try." So, taking the book, she asked: "In what condition is the interior of the globe?" and received the immediate answer from half the class at once: "The interior of the globe is in a condition of *igneous fusion*." Better exclusive object-teaching than such verbal recitations as that; and yet verbal reproduction, intelligently connected with more objective work, must always play a leading, and surely *the* leading, part in education. Our modern reformers, in their books, write too exclusively of the earliest years of the pupil. These lend themselves better to explicit treatment; and I myself, in dwelling so much upon the native impulses, and object-teaching, and anecdotes, and all that, have paid my tribute to the line of least resistance in describing. Yet away back in childhood we find the beginnings of purely intellectual curiosity, and the intelligence of abstract terms. The object-teaching is mainly to *launch* the pupils, with some concrete conceptions of the facts concerned, upon the more abstract ideas.

To hear some authorities on teaching, however, you would suppose that geography not only began, but ended with the school-yard and neighboring hill, that physics was one endless round of repeating the same sort of tedious weighing and measuring operation: whereas a very few examples are usually sufficient to set the imagination free on genuine lines, and then what the mind craves is more rapid, general, and abstract treatment. I heard a lady say that she had taken her child to the kindergarten, "but he is so bright that he saw through it immediately." Too many school children 'see' as immediately 'through' the namby-pamby attempts of the softer pedagogy to lubricate things for them, and make them interesting. Even they can enjoy abstractions, provided they be of the proper order; and it is a poor compliment to their rational appetite to think that anecdotes about little Tommies and little Jennies are the only kind of things their minds can digest.

But here, as elsewhere, it is a matter of more or less; and, in the last resort, the teacher's own tact is the only thing that can bring out the right effect. The great difficulty with abstractions is that of knowing just what meaning the pupil attaches to the terms he uses. The words may sound all right, but the meaning remains the child's own secret. So varied forms of words must be insisted on, to bring the secret out. And a strange secret does it often prove. A relative of mine was trying to explain to a little girl what was meant by 'the passive voice': "Suppose that you kill me: you who do the killing are in the active voice, and I, who am killed, am in the passive voice." "But how can you speak if you're killed?" said the child. "Oh, well, you may suppose that I am not yet quite dead!" The next day the child was asked, in class, to explain the passive voice, and said, "It's the kind of voice you speak with when you ain't quite dead."

In such a case as this the illustration ought to have been more varied. Every one's memory will probably furnish examples of the fantastic meaning which their childhood attached to certain verbal statements (in poetry often), and which their elders, not having any reason to suspect, never corrected. I remember being greatly moved emotionally at the age of eight by the ballad of Lord Ullin's Daughter. Yet I thought that the staining of the heather by the blood was the evil chiefly dreaded, and that, when the boatman said,

> "I'll row you o'er the ferry.
> It is not for your silver bright,
> But for your winsome lady,"

he was to receive the lady for his pay. Similarly, I recently found that one of my own children was reading (and accepting) a verse of Tennyson's In Memoriam as

> "Ring out the *food* of rich and poor,
>   Ring in *redness* to all mankind,"

and finding no inward difficulty.

The only safeguard against this sort of misconceiving is to insist on varied statement, and to bring the child's conceptions, wherever it be possible, to some sort of practical test.

Let us next pass to the subject of Apperception.

CHAPTER 14

Apperception

'APPERCEPTION' is a word which cuts a great figure in the pedagogics of the present day. Read, for example, this advertisement of a certain text-book, which I take from an educational journal:—

WHAT IS APPERCEPTION?

For an explanation of Apperception see Blank's PSYCHOLOGY, Vol. —— of the —— Education Series, just published.

The difference between Perception and Apperception is explained for the teacher in the preface to Blank's PSYCHOLOGY.

Many teachers are inquiring, "What is the meaning of Apperception in educational psychology?" Just the book for them is Blank's PSYCHOLOGY in which the idea was first expounded.

The most important idea in educational psychology is Apperception. The teacher

may find this expounded in Blank's PSY-
CHOLOGY. The idea of Apperception is
making a revolution in educational meth-
ods in Germany. It is explained in Blank's
PSYCHOLOGY, Vol. —— of the ——
Education Series, just published.

Blank's PSYCHOLOGY will be mailed
prepaid to any address on receipt of $1.00.

Such an advertisement is in sober earnest a disgrace to
all concerned; and such talk as it indulges in is the sort
of thing I had in view when I said at our first meeting
that the teachers were suffering at the present day from
a certain industrious mystification on the part of editors
and publishers. Perhaps the word 'apperception,' flourished
in their eyes and ears as it nowadays often is, embodies as
much of this mystification as any other single thing. The
conscientious young teacher is led to believe that it contains a recondite and portentous secret, by losing the true
inwardness of which her whole career may be shattered.
And yet, when she turns to the books and reads about it,
it seems so trivial and commonplace a matter,—meaning
nothing more than the manner in which we receive a
thing into our minds,—that she fears she must have missed
the point through the shallowness of her intelligence, and
goes about thereafter afflicted with a sense either of uncertainty or of stupidity, and in each case remaining
mortified at being so inadequate to her mission.

Now apperception is an extremely useful word in pedagogics, and offers a convenient name for a process to
which every teacher must frequently refer. But it verily
means nothing more than the act of taking a thing into
the mind. It corresponds to nothing peculiar or elementary
in psychology, being only one of the innumerable results
of the psychological process of association of ideas; and
psychology itself can easily dispense with the word, useful
as it may be in pedagogics.

The gist of the matter is this: Every impression that
comes in from without, be it a sentence which we hear,
an object of vision, or an effluvium which assails our nose,

no sooner enters our consciousness than it is drafted off in some determinate direction or other, making connection with the other materials already there, and finally producing what we call our reaction. The particular connections it strikes into are determined by our past experiences and the 'associations' of the present sort of impression with them. If, for instance, you hear me call out A, B, C, it is ten to one that you will react on the impression by inwardly or outwardly articulating D, E, F. The impression arouses its old associates; they go out to meet it; it is received by them, recognized by the mind as 'the beginning of the alphabet.' It is the fate of every impression thus to fall into a mind preoccupied with memories, ideas, and interests, and by these it is taken in. Educated as we already are, we never get an experience that remains for us completely nondescript: it always *reminds* of something similar in quality, or of some context that might have surrounded it before, and which it now in some way suggests. This mental escort which the mind supplies is drawn, of course, from the mind's ready-made stock. We *conceive* the impression in some definite way. We dispose of it according to our acquired possibilities, be they few or many, in the way of 'ideas.' This way of taking in the object is the process of apperception. The conceptions which meet and assimilate it are called by Herbart the 'apperceiving mass.' The apperceived impression is engulfed in this, and the result is a new field of consciousness, of which one part (and often a very small part) comes from the outer world, and another part (sometimes by far the largest) comes from the previous contents of the mind.

I think that you see plainly enough now that the process of apperception is what I called it a moment ago, a resultant of the association of ideas. The product is a sort of fusion of the new with the old, in which it is often impossible to distinguish the share of the two factors. For example, when we listen to a person speaking or read a page of print, much of what we think we see or hear is supplied from our memory. We overlook misprints, imagining the right letters, though we see the wrong ones;

and how little we actually hear, when we listen to speech, we realize when we go to a foreign theatre; for there what troubles us is not so much that we cannot understand what the actors say as that we cannot hear their words. The fact is that we hear quite as little under similar conditions at home, only our mind, being fuller of English verbal associations, supplies the requisite material for comprehension upon a much slighter auditory hint.

In all the apperceptive operations of the mind, a certain general law makes itself felt,—the law of economy. In admitting a new body of experience, we instinctively seek to disturb as little as possible our pre-existing stock of ideas. We always try to name a new experience in some way which will assimilate it to what we already know. We hate anything *absolutely* new, anything without any name, and for which a new name must be forged. So we take the nearest name, even though it be inappropriate. A child will call snow, when he sees it for the first time, sugar or white butterflies. The sail of a boat he calls a curtain; an egg in its shell, seen for the first time, he calls a pretty potato; an orange, a ball; a folding corkscrew, a pair of bad scissors. Caspar Hauser called the first geese he saw horses, and the Polynesians called Captain Cook's horses pigs. Mr. Rooper has written a little book on apperception, to which he gives the title of "A Pot of Green Feathers," that being the name applied to a pot of ferns by a child who had never seen ferns before.

In later life this economical tendency to leave the old undisturbed leads to what we know as 'old fogyism.' A new idea or a fact which would entail extensive rearrangement of the previous system of beliefs is always ignored or extruded from the mind in case it cannot be sophistically reinterpreted so as to tally harmoniously with the system. We have all conducted discussions with middle-aged people, overpowered them with our reasons, forced them to admit our contention, and a week later found them back as secure and constant in their old opinion as if they had never conversed with us at all. We call them old fogies; but there are young fogies, too. Old fogyism begins at a younger age than we think. I am almost afraid to say so, but I believe that in the majority of human beings it begins at about twenty-five.

In some of the books we find the various forms of apperception codified, and their subdivisions numbered and ticketed in tabular form in the way so delightful to the pedagogic eye. In one book which I remember reading there were sixteen different types of apperception discriminated from each other. There was associative apperception, subsumptive apperception, assimilative apperception, and others up to sixteen. It is needless to say that this is nothing but an exhibition of the crass artificiality which has always haunted psychology, and which perpetuates itself by lingering along, especially in these works which are advertised as 'written for the use of teachers.' The flowing life of the mind is sorted into parcels suitable for presentation in the recitation-room, and chopped up into supposed 'processes' with long Greek and Latin names, which in real life have no distinct existence.

There is no reason, if we are classing the different types of apperception, why we should stop at sixteen rather than sixteen hundred. There are as many types of apperception as there are possible ways in which an incoming experience may be reacted on by an individual mind. A little while ago, at Buffalo, I was the guest of a lady who, a fortnight before, had taken her seven-year-old boy for the first time to Niagara Falls. The child silently glared at the phenomenon until his mother, supposing him struck speechless by its sublimity, said, "Well, my boy, what do you think of it?" to which, "Is that the kind of spray I spray my nose with?" was the boy's only reply. That was his mode of apperceiving the spectacle. You may claim this as a particular type, and call it by the Greek name of rhinotherapeutical apperception, if you like; and, if you do, you will hardly be more trivial or artificial than are some of the authors of the books.

M. Perez, in one of his books on childhood, gives a good example of the different modes of apperception of the same phenomenon which are possible at different stages of individual experience. A dwelling-house took fire, and an infant in the family, witnessing the conflagration from the arms of his nurse, standing outside, expressed nothing but the liveliest delight at its brilliancy. But, when the bell of the fire-engine was heard approaching, the child was thrown by the sound into a paroxysm of fear, strange sounds being, as you know, very alarming to young children. In what opposite ways must the child's parents have apperceived the burning house and the engine respectively!

The self-same person, according to the line of thought he may be in, or to his emotional mood, will apperceive the same impression quite differently on different occasions. A medical or engineering expert retained on one side of a case will not apperceive the facts in the same way as if the other side had retained him. When people are at loggerheads about the interpretation of a fact, it usually shows that they have too few heads of classification to apperceive by; for, as a general thing, the fact of such a dispute is enough to show that neither one of their rival interpretations is a perfect fit. Both sides deal with the matter by approximation, squeezing it under the handiest or least disturbing conception: whereas it would, nine times out of ten, be better to enlarge their stock of ideas or invent some altogether new title for the phenomenon.

Thus, in biology, we used to have interminable discussion as to whether certain single-celled organisms were animals or vegetables, until Haeckel introduced the new apperceptive name of Protista, which ended the disputes. In law courts no *tertium quid* is recognized between insanity and sanity. If sane, a man is punished: if insane, acquitted; and it is seldom hard to find two experts who will take opposite views of his case. All the while, nature is more subtle than our doctors. Just as a room is neither dark nor light absolutely, but might be dark for a watch-maker's uses, and yet light enough to eat in or play in, so a man may be sane for some purposes and insane for others,—sane enough to be left at large, yet not sane enough to take care of his financial affairs. The word 'crank,' which became familiar at the time of Guiteau's trial, fulfilled the need of a *tertium quid*. The foreign terms 'déséquilibré,' 'hereditary degenerate,' and 'psycho-pathic' subject, have arisen in response to the same need.

The whole progress of our sciences goes on by the invention of newly forged technical names whereby to designate the newly remarked aspects of phenomena,—phenomena which could only be squeezed with violence into the pigeonholes of the earlier stock of conceptions. As time goes on, our vocabulary becomes thus ever more and more voluminous, having to keep up with the ever-growing multitude of our stock of apperceiving ideas.

In this gradual process of interaction between the new and the old, not only is the new modified and determined by the particular sort of old which apperceives it, but the apperceiving mass, the old itself, is modified by the particular kind of new which it assimilates. Thus, to take the stock German example of the child brought up in a house where there are no tables but square ones, 'table' means for him a thing in which square corners are essential. But, if he goes to a house where there are round tables and still calls them tables, his apperceiving notion 'table' acquires immediately a wider inward content. In this way, our conceptions are constantly dropping characters once supposed essential, and including others once supposed inadmissible. The extension of the notion 'beast' to porpoises and whales, of the notion 'organism' to society, are familiar examples of what I mean.

But be our conceptions adequate or inadequate, and be our stock of them large or small, they are all we have to work with. If an educated man is, as I said, a group of organized tendencies to conduct, what prompts the conduct is in every case the man's conception of the way in which to name and classify the actual emergency. The more adequate the stock of ideas, the more 'able' is the man, the more uniformly appropriate is his behavior likely to be. When later we take up the subject of the will, we shall see that the essential preliminary to every decision is the finding of the right *names* under which to class the proposed alternatives of conduct. He who has few names

is in so far forth an incompetent deliberator. The names
—and each name stands for a conception or idea—are our
instruments for handling our problems and solving our
dilemmas. Now, when we think of this, we are too apt
to forget an important fact, which is that in most human
beings the stock of names and concepts is mostly acquired
during the years of adolescence and the earliest years of
adult life. I probably shocked you a moment ago by saying that most men begin to be old fogies at the age of
twenty-five. It is true that a grown-up adult keeps gaining
well into middle age a great knowledge of details, and
a great acquaintance with individual cases connected with
his profession or business life. In this sense, his conceptions
increase during a very long period; for his knowledge grows
more extensive and minute. But the larger categories of
conception, the sorts of thing, and wider classes of relation between things, of which we take cognizance, are
all got into the mind at a comparatively youthful date. Few
men ever do acquaint themselves with the principles of a
new science after even twenty-five. If you do not study
political economy in college, it is a thousand to one that its
main conceptions will remain unknown to you through
life. Similarly with biology, similarly with electricity. What
percentage of persons now fifty years old have any definite
conception whatever of a dynamo, or how the trolley-cars
are made to run? Surely, a small fraction of one per cent.
But the boys in colleges are all acquiring these conceptions.

There is a sense of infinite potentiality in us all, when
young, which makes some of us draw up lists of books we
intend to read hereafter, and makes most of us think that
we can easily acquaint ourselves with all sorts of things
which we are now neglecting by studying them out hereafter in the intervals of leisure of our business lives. Such
good intentions are hardly ever carried out. The conceptions acquired before thirty remain usually the only ones
we ever gain. Such exceptional cases of perpetually self-
renovating youth as Mr. Gladstone's only prove, by the
admiration they awaken, the universality of the rule. And
it may well solemnize a teacher, and confirm in him a

healthy sense of the importance of his mission, to feel how exclusively dependent upon his present ministrations in the way of imparting conceptions the pupil's future life is probably bound to be.

CHAPTER 15

The Will

SINCE mentality terminates naturally in outward conduct, the final chapter in psychology has to be the chapter on the will. But the word 'will' can be used in a broader and in a narrower sense. In the broader sense, it designates our entire capacity for impulsive and active life, including our instinctive reactions and those forms of behavior that have become secondarily automatic and semi-unconscious through frequent repetition. In the narrower sense, acts of will are such acts only as cannot be inattentively performed. A distinct idea of what they are, and a deliberate *fiat* on the mind's part, must precede their execution.

Such acts are often characterized by hesitation, and accompanied by a feeling, altogether peculiar, of resolve, a feeling which may or may not carry with it a further feeling of effort. In my earlier talks, I said so much of our impulsive tendencies that I will restrict myself in what follows to volition in this narrower sense of the term.

All our deeds were considered by the early psychologists to be due to a peculiar faculty called the will, without whose fiat action could not occur. Thoughts and impressions, being intrinsically inactive, were supposed to produce conduct only through the intermediation of this superior

agent. Until they twitched its coat-tails, so to speak, no
outward behavior could occur. This doctrine was long ago
exploded by the discovery of the phenomena of reflex
action, in which sensible impressions, as you know, produce
movement immediately and of themselves. The doctrine
may also be considered exploded as far as ideas go.

The fact is that there is no sort of consciousness whatever, be it sensation, feeling, or idea, which does not
directly and of itself tend to discharge into some motor
effect. The motor effect need not always be an outward
stroke of behavior. It may be only an alteration of the
heart-beats or breathing, or a modification in the distribution of blood, such as blushing or turning pale; or else a
secretion of tears, or what not. But, in any case, it is
there in some shape when any consciousness is there; and
a belief as fundamental as any in modern psychology is the
belief at last attained that conscious processes of any sort,
conscious processes merely as such, *must* pass over into
motion, open or concealed.

The least complicated case of this tendency is the case
of a mind possessed by only a single idea. If that idea
be of an object connected with a native impulse, the impulse will immediately proceed to discharge. If it be the
idea of a movement, the movement will occur. Such a case
of action from a single idea has been distinguished from
more complex cases by the name of 'ideo-motor' action,
meaning action without express decision or effort. Most
of the habitual actions to which we are trained are of
this ideo-motor sort. We perceive, for instance, that the
door is open, and we rise and shut it; we perceive some
raisins in a dish before us, and extend our hand and carry
one of them to our mouth without interrupting the conversation; or, when lying in bed, we suddenly think that
we shall be late for breakfast, and instantly we get up
with no particular exertion or resolve. All the ingrained
procedures by which life is carried on—the manners and
customs, dressing and undressing, acts of salutation, etc.—
are executed in this semi-automatic way unhesitatingly and
efficiently, the very outermost margin of consciousness

seeming to be concerned in them, while the focus may be occupied with widely different things.

But now turn to a more complicated case. Suppose two thoughts to be in the mind together, of which one, A, taken alone, would discharge itself in a certain action, but of which the other, B, suggests an action of a different sort, or a consequence of the first action calculated to make us shrink. The psychologists now say that the second idea, B, will probably arrest or *inhibit* the motor effects of the first idea, A. One word, then, about 'inhibition' in general, to make this particular case more clear.

One of the most interesting discoveries of physiology was the discovery, made simultaneously in France and Germany fifty years ago, that nerve currents do not only start muscles into action, but may check action already going on or keep it from occurring as it otherwise might. *Nerves of arrest* were thus distinguished alongside of motor nerves. The pneumogastric nerve, for example, if stimulated, arrests the movements of the heart: the splanchnic nerve arrests those of the intestines, if already begun. But it soon appeared that this was too narrow a way of looking at the matter, and that arrest is not so much the specific function of certain nerves as a general function which any part of the nervous system may exert upon other parts under the appropriate conditions. The higher centres, for example, seem to exert a constant inhibitive influence on the excitability of those below. The reflexes of an animal with its hemispheres wholly or in part removed become exaggerated. You all know that common reflex in dogs, whereby, if you scratch the animal's side, the corresponding hind leg will begin to make scratching movements, usually in the air. Now in dogs with mutilated hemispheres this scratching reflex is so incessant that, as Goltz first described them, the hair gets all worn off their sides. In idiots, the functions of the hemispheres being largely in abeyance, the lower impulses, not inhibited, as they would be in normal human beings, often express themselves in most odious ways. You know also how any higher emotional tendency will quench a lower one. Fear arrests appetite, maternal love annuls fear, respect checks sensuality, and the like; and in the more subtle manifestations of the moral life, whenever an ideal stirring is suddenly quickened into intensity, it is as if the whole scale of values of our motives changed its equilibrium. The force of old temptations vanishes, and what a moment ago was impossible is now not only possible, but easy, because of their inhibition. This has been well called the 'expulsive power of the higher emotion.'

It is easy to apply this notion of inhibition to the case of our ideational processes. I am lying in bed, for example, and think it is time to get up; but alongside of this thought there is present to my mind a realization of the extreme coldness of the morning and the pleasantness of the warm bed. In such a situation the motor consequences of the first idea are blocked; and I may remain for half an hour or more with the two ideas oscillating before me in a kind of deadlock, which is what we call the state of hesitation or deliberation. In a case like this the deliberation can be resolved and the decision reached in either of two ways:—

(1) I may forget for a moment the thermometric conditions, and then the idea of getting up will immediately discharge into act: I shall suddenly find that I have got up—or

(2) Still mindful of the freezing temperature, the thought of the duty of rising may become so pungent that it determines action in spite of inhibition. In the latter case, I have a sense of energetic moral effort, and consider that I have done a virtuous act.

All cases of wilful action properly so called, of choice after hesitation and deliberation, may be conceived after one of these latter patterns. So you see that volition, in the narrower sense, takes place only when there are a number of conflicting systems of ideas, and depends on our having a complex field of consciousness. The interesting thing to note is the extreme delicacy of the inhibitive machinery. A strong and urgent motor idea in the focus may be neutralized and made inoperative by the presence of the very faintest contradictory idea in the margin. For instance, I hold out my forefinger, and with closed eyes try to realize as vividly as possible that I hold a revolver in my hand and am pulling the trigger. I can even now fairly feel my finger quivering with the tendency to contract; and, if it were hitched to a recording apparatus, it would certainly betray its state of tension by registering incipient movements. Yet it does not actually crook, and the movement of pulling the trigger is not performed. Why not? Simply because, all concentrated though I am upon the idea of the movement, I nevertheless also realize the total conditions of the experiment, and in the back of my mind, so to speak, or in its fringe and margin, have the simultaneous idea that the movement is not to take place. The mere presence of that marginal intention, without effort, urgency, or emphasis, or any special reinforcement from my attention, suffices to the inhibitive effect.

And this is why so few of the ideas that flit through our minds do, in point of fact, produce their motor consequences. Life would be a curse and a care for us if every fleeting fancy were to do so. Abstractly, the law of ideo-motor action is true; but in the concrete our fields of consciousness are always so complex that the inhibiting margin keeps the centre inoperative most of the time. In all this, you see, I speak as if ideas by their mere presence or absence determined behavior, and as if between the ideas themselves on the one hand and the conduct on the other there were no room for any third intermediate principle of activity, like that called 'the will.'

If you are struck by the materialistic or fatalistic doctrines which seem to follow this conception, I beg you to suspend your judgment for a moment, as I shall soon have something more to say about the matter. But, meanwhile yielding one's self to the mechanical conception of the psychophysical organism, nothing is easier than to indulge in a picture of the fatalistic character of human life. Man's conduct appears as the mere resultant of all his various impulsions and inhibitions. One object, by its presence, makes us act: another object checks our action. Feelings aroused and ideas suggested by objects sway us one way and another: emotions complicate the game by their mutual inhibitive effects, the higher abolishing the lower or perhaps being itself swept away. The life in all this becomes prudential and moral; but the psychologic agents in the drama may be described, you see, as nothing but the 'ideas' themselves,—ideas for the whole system of which what we call the 'soul' or 'character' or 'will' of the person is nothing but a collective name. As Hume said, the ideas are themselves the actors, the stage, the theatre, the spectators, and the play. This is the so-called 'associationist' psychology, brought down to its radical expression: it is useless to ignore its power as a conception. Like all conceptions, when they become clear and lively enough, this conception has a strong tendency to impose itself upon belief; and psychologists trained on biological lines usually adopt it as the last word of science on the subject. No one can have an adequate notion of modern psychological theory unless he has at some time apprehended this view in the full force of its simplicity.

Let us humor it for a while, for it has advantages in the way of exposition.

Voluntary action, then, is at all times a resultant of the compounding of our impulsions with our inhibitions.

From this it immediately follows that there will be two types of will, in one of which impulsions will predominate, in the other inhibitions. We may speak of them, if you like, as the precipitate and the obstructed will, respectively. When fully pronounced, they are familiar to everybody. The extreme example of the precipitate will is the maniac: his ideas discharge into action so rapidly, his associative processes are so extravagantly lively, that inhibitions have no time to arrive, and he says and does whatever pops into his head without a moment of hesitation.

Certain melancholiacs furnish the extreme example of the over-inhibited type. Their minds are cramped in a fixed emotion of fear or helplessness, their ideas confined to the one thought that for them life is impossible. So they show a condition of perfect 'abulia,' or inability to will or act. They cannot change their posture or speech or execute the simplest command.

The different races of men show different temperaments in this regard. The Southern races are commonly accounted the more impulsive and precipitate: the English race, especially our New England branch of it, is supposed to be all sicklied over with repressive forms of self-consciousness, and condemned to express itself through a jungle of scruples and checks.

The highest form of character, however, abstractly considered, must be full of scruples and inhibitions. But action, in such a character, far from being paralyzed, will succeed in energetically keeping on its way, sometimes overpowering the resistances, sometimes steering along the line where they lie thinnest.

Just as our extensor muscles act most truly when a simultaneous contraction of the flexors guides and steadies them; so the mind of him whose fields of consciousness are complex, and who, with the reasons for the action, sees the reasons against it, and yet, instead of being palsied, acts in the way that takes the whole field into consideration,— so, I say, is such a mind the ideal sort of mind that we should seek to reproduce in our pupils. Purely impulsive action, or action that proceeds to extremities regardless of consequences, on the other hand, is the easiest action in the world, and the lowest in type. Any one can show energy, when made quite reckless. An Oriental despot requires but little ability: as long as he lives, he succeeds, for he has absolutely his own way; and, when the world can no longer endure the horror of him, he is assassinated. But not to proceed immediately to extremities, to be still able to act energetically under an array of inhibitions,— that indeed is rare and difficult. Cavour, when urged to proclaim martial law in 1859, refused to do so, saying: "Any one can govern in that way. I will be constitutional."

Your parliamentary rulers, your Lincoln, your Gladstone, are the strongest type of man, because they accomplish results under the most intricate possible conditions. We think of Napoleon Bonaparte as a colossal monster of will-power, and truly enough he was so. But, from the point of view of the psychological machinery, it would be hard to say whether he or Gladstone was the larger volitional quantity; for Napoleon disregarded all the usual inhibitions, and Gladstone, passionate as he was, scrupulously considered them in his statesmanship.

A familiar example of the paralyzing power of scruples is the inhibitive effect of conscientiousness upon conversation. Nowhere does conversation seem to have flourished as brilliantly as in France during the last century. But, if we read old French memoirs, we see how many brakes of scrupulosity which tie our tongues to-day were then removed. Where mendacity, treachery, obscenity, and malignity find unhampered expression, talk can be brilliant indeed. But its flame waxes dim where the mind is stitched all over with conscientious fear of violating the moral and social proprieties.

The teacher often is confronted in the schoolroom with an abnormal type of will, which we may call the 'balky will.' Certain children, if they do not succeed in doing a thing immediately, remain completely inhibited in regard to it: it becomes literally impossible for them to understand it if it be an intellectual problem, or to do it if it be an outward operation, as long as this particular inhibited condition lasts. Such children are usually treated as sinful, and are punished; or else the teacher pits his or her will against the child's will, considering that the latter must be 'broken.' "Break your child's will, in order that it may not perish," wrote John Wesley. "Break its will as soon as it can speak plainly—or even before it can speak at all. It should be forced to do as it is told, even if you have to whip it ten times running. Break its will, in order that its soul may live." Such will-breaking is always a scene with a great deal of nervous wear and tear on both sides, a bad state of feeling left behind it, and the victory not always with the would-be will-breaker.

When a situation of the kind is once fairly developed, and the child is all tense and excited inwardly, nineteen times out of twenty it is best for the teacher to apperceive the case as one of neural pathology rather than as one of moral culpability. So long as the inhibiting sense of impossibility remains in the child's mind, he will continue unable to get beyond the obstacle. The aim of the teacher should then be to make him simply forget. Drop the subject for the time, divert the mind to something else: then, leading the pupil back by some circuitous line of association, spring it on him again before he has time to recognize it, and as likely as not he will go over it now without any difficulty. It is in no other way that we overcome balkiness in a horse: we divert his attention, do something to his nose or ear, lead him round in a circle, and thus get him over a place where flogging would only have made him more invincible. A tactful teacher will never let these strained situations come up at all.

You perceive now, my friends, what your general or abstract duty is as teachers. Although you have to generate in your pupils a large stock of ideas, any one of which may be inhibitory, yet you must also see to it that no habitual hesitancy or paralysis of the will ensues, and that the pupil still retains his power of vigorous action. Psychology can state your problem in these terms, but you see how impotent she is to furnish the elements of its practical solution. When all is said and done, and your best efforts are made, it will probably remain true that the result will depend more on a certain native tone or temper in the pupil's psychological constitution than on anything else. Some persons appear to have a naturally poor focalization of the field of consciousness; and in such persons actions hang slack, and inhibitions seem to exert peculiarly easy sway.

But let us now close in a little more closely on this

matter of the education of the will. Your task is to build up a *character* in your pupils; and a character, as I have so often said, consists in an organized set of habits of reaction. Now of what do such habits of reaction themselves consist? They consist of tendencies to act characteristically when certain ideas possess us, and to refrain characteristically when possessed by other ideas.

Our volitional habits depend, then, first, on what the stock of ideas is which we have; and, second, on the habitual coupling of the several ideas with action or inaction respectively. How is it when an alternative is presented to you for choice, and you are uncertain what you ought to do? You first hesitate, and then you deliberate. And in what does your deliberation consist? It consists in trying to apperceive the case successively by a number of different ideas, which seem to fit it more or less, until at last you hit on one which seems to fit it exactly. If that be an idea which is a customary forerunner of action in you, which enters into one of your maxims of positive behavior, your hesitation ceases, and you act immediately. If, on the other .hand, it be an idea which carries inaction as its habitual result, if it ally itself with *prohibition*, then you unhesitatingly refrain. The problem is, you see, to find the right idea or conception for the case. This search for the right conception may take days or weeks.

I spoke as if the action were easy when the conception once is found. Often it is so, but it may be otherwise; and, when it is otherwise, we find ourselves at the very centre of a moral situation, into which I should now like you to look with me a little nearer.

The proper conception, the true head of classification, may be hard to attain; or it may be one with which we have contracted no settled habits of action. Or, again, the action to which it would prompt may be dangerous and difficult; or else inaction may appear deadly cold and negative when our impulsive feeling is hot. In either of these latter cases it is hard to hold the right idea steadily enough before the attention to let it exert its adequate effects. Whether it be stimulative or inhibitive, it is *too reasonable* for us; and the more instinctive passional propensity then tends to extrude it from our consideration. We shy away from the thought of it. It twinkles and goes out the moment it appears in the margin of our consciousness; and we need a resolute effort of voluntary attention to drag it into the focus of the field, and to keep it there long enough for its associative and motor effects to be exerted. Every one knows only too well how the mind flinches from looking at considerations hostile to the reigning mood of feeling.

Once brought, however, in this way to the centre of the field of consciousness, and held there, the reasonable idea will exert these effects inevitably; for the laws of connection between our consciousness and our nervous system provide for the action then taking place. Our moral effort, properly so called, terminates in our holding fast to the appropriate idea.

If, then, you are asked, *"In what does a moral act consist* when reduced to its simplest and most elementary form?"* you can make only one reply. You can say that *it consists in the effort of attention by which we hold fast to an idea* which but for that effort of attention would be driven out of the mind by the other psychological tendencies that are there. *To think,* in short, is the secret of will, just as it is the secret of memory.

This comes out very clearly in the kind of excuse which we most frequently hear from persons who find themselves confronted by the sinfulness or harmfulness of some part of their behavior. "I never *thought,"* they say. "I never *thought* how mean the action was, I never *thought* of these abominable consequences." And what do we retort when they say this? We say: "Why *didn't* you think? What were you there for but to think?" And we read them a moral lecture on their irreflectiveness.

The hackneyed example of moral deliberation is the case of an habitual drunkard under temptation. He has made a resolve to reform, but he is now solicited again by the bottle. His moral triumph or failure literally consists in his

finding the right *name* for the case. If he says that it is
a case of not wasting good liquor already poured out, or a
case of not being churlish and unsociable when in the
midst of friends, or a case of learning something at last
about a brand of whiskey which he never met before, or
a case of celebrating a public holiday, or a case of stimu-
lating himself to a more energetic resolve in favor of absti-
nence than any he has ever yet made, then he is lost.
His choice of the wrong name seals his doom. But if, in
spite of all the plausible good names with which his thirsty
fancy so copiously furnishes him, he unwaveringly clings
to the truer bad name, and apperceives the case as that
of "being a drunkard, being a drunkard, being a drunkard,"
his feet are planted on the road to salvation. He saves
himself by thinking rightly.

Thus are your pupils to be saved: first, by the stock of
ideas with which you furnish them; second, by the amount
of voluntary attention that they can exert in holding to
the right ones, however unpalatable; and, third, by the
several habits of acting definitely on these latter to which
they have been successfully trained.

In all this the power of voluntarily attending is the
point of the whole procedure. Just as a balance turns on
its knife-edges, so on it our moral destiny turns. You remember that, when we were talking of the subject of attention, we discovered how much more intermittent and
brief our acts of voluntary attention are than is commonly
supposed. If they were all summed together, the time that
they occupy would cover an almost incredibly small portion of our lives. But I also said, you will remember, that
their brevity was not in proportion to their significance,
and that I should return to the subject again. So I return
to it now. It is not the mere size of a thing which constitutes its importance: it is its position in the organism to
which it belongs. Our acts of voluntary attention, brief
and fitful as they are, are nevertheless momentous and
critical, determining us, as they do, to higher or lower
destinies. The exercise of voluntary attention in the schoolroom must therefore be counted one of the most important

points of training that take place there; and the first-rate teacher, by the keenness of the remoter interests which he is able to awaken, will provide abundant opportunities for its occurrence. I hope that you appreciate this now without any further explanation.

I have been accused of holding up before you, in the course of these talks, a mechanical and even a materialistic view of the mind. I have called it an organism and a machine. I have spoken of its reaction on the environment as the essential thing about it; and I have referred this, either openly or implicitly, to the construction of the nervous system. I have, in consequence, received notes from some of you, begging me to be more explicit on this point; and to let you know frankly whether I am a complete materialist, or not.

Now in these lectures I wish to be strictly practical and useful, and to keep free from all speculative complications. Nevertheless, I do not wish to leave any ambiguity about my own position; and I will therefore say, in order to avoid all misunderstanding, that in no sense do I count myself a materialist. I cannot see how such a thing as our consciousness can possibly be *produced* by a nervous machinery, though I can perfectly well see how, if 'ideas' do accompany the workings of the machinery, the *order* of the ideas might very well follow exactly the *order* of the machine's operations. Our habitual associations of ideas, trains of thought, and sequences of action, might thus be consequences of the succession of currents in our nervous systems. And the possible stock of ideas which a man's free spirit would have to choose from might depend exclusively on the native and acquired powers of his brain. If this were all, we might indeed adopt the fatalist conception which I sketched for you but a short while ago. Our ideas would be determined by brain currents, and these by purely mechanical laws.

But, after what we have just seen,—namely, the part played by voluntary attention in volition,—a belief in free will and purely spiritual causation is still open to us. The duration and amount of this attention *seem* within certain limits indeterminate. We *feel* as if we could make it really more or less, and as if our free action in this regard were a genuine critical point in nature,—a point on which our destiny and that of others might hinge. The whole question of free will concentrates itself, then, at this same small point. "Is or is not the appearance of indetermination at this point an illusion?"

It is plain that such a question can be decided only by general analogies, and not by accurate observations. The free-willist believes the appearance to be a reality: the determinist believes that it is an illusion. I myself hold with the free-willists,—not because I cannot conceive the fatalist theory clearly, or because I fail to understand its plausibility, but simply because, if free will *were* true, it would be absurd to have the belief in it fatally forced on our acceptance. Considering the inner fitness of things, one would rather think that the very first act of a will endowed with freedom should be to sustain the belief in the freedom itself. I accordingly believe freely in my freedom; I do so with the best of scientific consciences, knowing that the predetermination of the amount of my effort of attention can never receive objective proof, and hoping that, whether you follow my example in this respect or not, it will at least make you see that such psychological and psychophysical theories as I hold do not necessarily force a man to become a fatalist or a materialist.

Let me say one more final word now about the will, and therewith conclude both that important subject and these lectures.

There are two types of will. There are also two types of inhibition. We may call them inhibition by repression or by negation, and inhibition by substitution, respectively. The difference between them is that, in the case of inhibition by repression, both the inhibited idea and the inhibiting idea, the impulsive idea and the idea that negates it, remain along with each other in consciousness, producing a certain inward strain or tension there: whereas, in inhibition by substitution, the inhibiting idea supersedes altogether the idea which it inhibits, and the latter quickly vanishes from the field.

For instance, your pupils are wandering in mind, are listening to a sound outside the window, which presently grows interesting enough to claim all their attention. You can call the latter back again by bellowing at them not to listen to those sounds, but to keep their minds on their books or on what you are saying. And, by thus keeping them conscious that your eye is sternly on them, you may produce a good effect. But it will be a wasteful effect and an inferior effect; for the moment you relax your super-vision the attractive disturbance, always there soliciting their curiosity, will overpower them, and they will be just as they were before: whereas, if, without saying any-thing about the street disturbances, you open a counter-attraction by starting some very interesting talk or demon-stration yourself, they will altogether forget the distracting incident, and without any effort follow you along. There are many interests that can never be inhibited by the way of negation. To a man in love, for example, it is literally impossible, by any effort of will, to annul his passion. But let 'some new planet swim into his ken,' and the former idol will immediately cease to engross his mind.

It is clear that in general we ought, whenever we can, to employ the method of inhibition by substitution. He whose life is based upon the word 'no,' who tells the truth because a lie is wicked, and who has constantly to grapple with his envious and cowardly and mean propensities, is in an inferior situation in every respect to what he would be if the love of truth and magnanimity positively possessed him from the outset, and he felt no inferior temptations. Your born gentleman is certainly, for this world's purposes, a more valuable being than your "Crump, with his grunting resistance to his native devils," even though in God's sight the latter may, as the Catholic theologians say, be rolling up great stores of 'merit.'

Spinoza long ago wrote in his Ethics that anything that a man can avoid under the notion that it is bad he may also avoid under the notion that something else is good. He who habitually acts *sub specie mali*, under the negative notion, the notion of the bad, is called a slave by Spinoza. To him who acts habitually under the notion of good he gives the name of freeman. See to it now, I beg you, that you make freemen of your pupils by habituating them to act, whenever possible, under the notion of a good. Get them habitually to tell the truth, not so much through showing them the wickedness of lying as by arousing their enthusiasm for honor and veracity. Wean them from their native cruelty by imparting to them some of your own positive sympathy with an animal's inner springs of joy. And, in the lessons which you may be legally obliged to conduct upon the bad effects of alcohol, lay less stress than the books do on the drunkard's stomach, kidneys, nerves, and social miseries, and more on the blessings of having an organism kept in lifelong possession of its full youthful elasticity by a sweet, sound blood, to which stimulants and narcotics are unknown, and to which the morning sun and air and dew will daily come as sufficiently powerful intoxicants.

I have now ended these talks. If to some of you the things I have said seem obvious or trivial, it is possible that they may appear less so when, in the course of a year or two, you find yourselves noticing and apperceiving events in the schoolroom a little differently, in consequence of some of the conceptions I have tried to make more clear. I cannot but think that to apperceive your pupil as a little sensitive, impulsive, associative, and reactive organism, partly fated and partly free, will lead to a better intelligence of all his ways. Understand him, then, as such a subtle little piece of machinery. And if, in addition, you can also see him *sub specie boni*, and love him as well, you will be in the best possible position for becoming perfect teachers.

TALKS TO STUDENTS

CHAPTER 1

The Gospel of Relaxation

I wish in the following hour to take certain psychological doctrines and show their practical applications to mental hygiene,—to the hygiene of our American life more particularly. Our people, especially in academic circles, are turning towards psychology nowadays with great expectations; and, if psychology is to justify them, it must be by showing fruits in the pedagogic and therapeutic lines.

The reader may possibly have heard of a peculiar theory of the emotions, commonly referred to in psychological literature as the Lange-James theory. According to this theory, our emotions are mainly due to those organic stirrings that are aroused in us in a reflex way by the stimulus of the exciting object or situation. An emotion of fear, for example, or surprise, is not a direct effect of the object's presence on the mind, but an effect of that still earlier effect, the bodily commotion which the object suddenly excites; so that, were this bodily commotion suppressed, we should not so much *feel* fear as call the situation fearful; we should not feel surprise, but coldly recognize that the object was indeed astonishing. One enthusiast has even gone so far as to say that when we feel sorry it is because we weep, when we feel afraid it is because we run away, and not conversely. Some of you may perhaps be acquainted with the paradoxical formula. Now, whatever exaggeration may possibly lurk in this account of our emotions (and I doubt myself whether the exaggeration be very great), it is certain that the main core of it is true, and that the mere giving way to tears, for example, or to the outward expression of an anger-fit, will result for the moment in making the inner grief or anger more acutely felt. There is, accordingly, no better known or more generally useful precept in the moral training of youth, or in one's personal self-discipline, than that which bids us pay primary attention to what we do and express, and not to care too much for what we feel. If we only check a cowardly impulse in time, for example, or if we only *don't* strike the blow or rip out with the complaining or insulting word that we shall regret as long as we live, our feelings themselves will presently be the calmer and better, with no particular guidance from us on their own account. Action seems to follow feeling, but really action and feeling go together; and by regulating the action, which is under the more direct control of the will, we can indirectly regulate the feeling, which is not.

Thus the sovereign voluntary path to cheerfulness, if our spontaneous cheerfulness be lost, is to sit up cheerfully, to look round cheerfully, and to act and speak as if cheerfulness were already there. If such conduct does not make you soon feel cheerful, nothing else on that occasion can. So to feel brave, act as if we *were* brave, use all our will to that end, and a courage-fit will very likely replace the fit of fear. Again, in order to feel kindly toward a person to whom we have been inimical, the only way is more or less deliberately to smile, to make sympathetic inquiries, and to force ourselves to say genial things. One hearty laugh together will bring enemies into a closer communion of heart than hours spent on both sides in inward wrestling with the mental demon of uncharitable feeling. To wrestle with a bad feeling only pins our attention on it, and keeps it still fastened in the mind: whereas, if we act as if from some better feeling, the old bad feeling soon folds its tent like an Arab, and silently steals away.

The best manuals of religious devotion accordingly reiterate the maxim that we must let our feelings go, and pay no regard to them whatever. In an admirable and widely successful little book called 'The Christian's Secret of a Happy Life,' by Mrs. Hannah Whitall Smith, I find this lesson on· almost every page. *Act* faithfully, and you really have faith, no matter how cold and even how dubious you may feel. "It is your purpose God looks at," writes Mrs. Smith, "not your feelings about that purpose; and your purpose, or will, is therefore the only thing you need attend to. . . . Let your emotions come or let them go, just as God pleases, and make no account of them either way. . . . They really have nothing to do with the matter. They are not the indicators of your spiritual state, but are merely the indicators of your temperament or of your present physical condi· tion."

But you all know these facts already, so I need no longer press them on your attention. From our acts and from our attitudes ceaseless inpouring currents of sensation come, which help to determine from moment to moment what our inner states shall be: that is a fundamental law of psychology which I will therefore proceed to assume.

A Viennese neurologist of considerable reputation has recently written about the *Binnenleben*, as he terms it, or buried life of human beings. No doctor, this writer says, can get into really profitable relations with a nervous patient until he gets some sense of what the patient's *Binnenleben* is, of the sort of unuttered inner atmosphere in which his consciousness dwells alone with the secrets of its prison-house. This inner personal tone is what we can't communicate or describe articulately to others; but the wraith and ghost of it, so to speak, are often what our friends and intimates feel as our most characteristic quality. In the unhealthy-minded, apart from all sorts of old regrets, ambitions checked by shames and aspirations obstructed by timidities, it consists mainly of bodily discomforts not distinctly localized by the sufferer, but breeding a general self-mistrust and sense that things are not as they should be with him. Half the thirst for alcohol that exists in the world exists simply because alcohol acts as a temporary anæsthetic and effacer to all these morbid feelings that never ought to be in a human being at all. In the healthy-minded, on the contrary, there are no fears or shames to discover; and the sensations that pour in from the organism only help to swell the general vital sense of security and readiness for anything that may turn up.

Consider, for example, the effects of a well-toned *motor-apparatus*, nervous and muscular, on our general personal self-consciousness, the sense of elasticity and efficiency that results. They tell us that in Norway the life of the women has lately been entirely revolutionized by the new order of muscular feelings with which the use of the *ski*, or long snow-shoes, as a sport for both sexes, has made the women acquainted. Fifteen years ago the Norwegian women were even more than the women of other lands votaries of the old-fashioned ideal of femininity, 'the domestic angel,' the 'gentle and refining influence' sort of thing. Now these sedentary fireside tabby-cats of Norway have been trained, they say, by the snow-shoes into lithe and audacious creatures, for whom no night is too dark or height too giddy, and who are not only saying good-bye to the traditional feminine pallor and delicacy of constitution, but actually taking the lead in every educational and social reform. I cannot but think that the tennis and tramping and skating habits and the bicycle-craze which are so rapidly extending among our dear sisters and daughters in this country are going also to lead to a sounder and heartier moral tone, which will send its tonic breath through all our American life.

I hope that here in America more and more the ideal of the well-trained and vigorous body will be maintained neck by neck with that of the well-trained and vigorous mind as the two coequal halves of the higher education for men and women alike. The strength of the British Empire lies in the strength of character of the individual Englishman, taken all alone by himself. And that strength, I am persuaded, is perennially nourished and kept up by nothing so much as by the national worship, in which all classes meet, of athletic outdoor life and sport.

I recollect, years ago, reading a certain work by an American doctor on hygiene and the laws of life and the type of future humanity. I have forgotten its author's name and its title, but I remember well an awful prophecy that it contained about the future of our muscular system. Human perfection, the writer said, means ability to cope with the environment; but the environment will more and more require mental power from us, and less and less will ask for bare brute strength. Wars will cease, machines will do all our heavy work, man will become more and more a mere director of nature's energies, and less and less an exerter of energy on his own account. So that, if the *homo sapiens* of the future can only digest his food and think, what need will he have of well-developed muscles at all? And why, pursued this writer, should we not even now be satisfied with a more delicate and intellectual type of beauty than that which pleased our ancestors? Nay, I have heard a fanciful friend make a still further advance in this 'new-man' direction. With our future food, he says, itself prepared in liquid form from the chemical elements of the atmosphere, pepsinated or half-digested in advance, and sucked up through a glass tube from a tin can, what need shall we have of teeth, or stomachs even? They may go, along with our muscles and our physical courage, while, challenging ever more and more our proper admiration, will grow the gigantic domes of our crania, arching over our spectacled eyes, and animating our flexible little lips to those floods of learned and ingenious talk which will constitute our most congenial occupation.

I am sure that your flesh creeps at this apocalyptic vision. Mine certainly did so; and I cannot believe that our muscular vigor will ever be a superfluity. Even if the day ever dawns in which it will not be needed for fighting the old heavy battles against Nature, it will still always be needed to furnish the background of sanity, serenity, and cheerfulness to life, to give moral elasticity to our disposition, to round off the wiry edge of our fretfulness, and make us good-humored and easy of approach. Weakness is too apt to be what the doctors call irritable weakness. And that blessed internal peace and confidence, that *acquiescentia in seipso,* as Spinoza used to call it, that wells up from every part of the body of a muscularly well-trained human being, and soaks the indwelling soul of him with satisfaction, is, quite apart from every consideration of its mechanical utility, an element of spiritual hygiene of supreme significance.

And now let me go a step deeper into mental hygiene, and try to enlist your insight and sympathy in a cause which I believe is one of paramount patriotic importance to us Yankees. Many years ago a Scottish medical man, Dr. Clouston, a mad-doctor as they call him there, or what we should call an asylum physician (the most eminent one in Scotland), visited this country, and said something that has remained in my memory ever since. "You Americans," he said, "wear too much expression on your faces. You are living like an army with all its reserves engaged in action. The duller countenances of the British population betoken a better scheme of life. They suggest stores of reserved nervous force to fall back upon, if any occasion should arise that requires it. This inexcitability, this presence at all times of power not used, I regard," continued Dr. Clouston, "as the great safeguard of our British people. The other thing in you gives me a sense of insecurity, and you ought somehow to tone yourselves down. You really do carry too much expression, you take too intensely the trivial moments of life."

Now Dr. Clouston is a trained reader of the secrets of the soul as expressed upon the countenance, and the observation of his which I quote seems to me to mean a great deal. And all Americans who stay in Europe long enough to get accustomed to the spirit that reigns and expresses itself there, so unexcitable as compared with ours, make a similar observation when they return to their native shores. They find a wild-eyed look upon their compatriots' faces, either of too desperate eagerness and anxiety or of too intense responsiveness and good-will. It is hard to say whether the men or the women show it most. It is true that we do not all feel about it as Dr. Clouston felt. Many of us, far from deploring it, admire it. We say: "What intelligence it shows! How different from the stolid cheeks, the codfish eyes, the slow, inanimate demeanor we have been seeing in the British Isles!" Intensity, rapidity, vivacity of appearance, are indeed with us something of a nationally accepted ideal; and the medical notion of 'irritable weakness' is not the first thing suggested by them to our mind, as it was to Dr. Clouston's. In a weekly paper not very long ago I remember reading a story in which, after describing the beauty and interest of the heroine's personality, the author summed up her charms by saying that to all who looked upon her an impression as of 'bottled lightning' was irresistibly conveyed.

Bottled lightning, in truth, is one of our American ideals, even of a young girl's character! Now it is most ungracious, and it may seem to some persons unpatriotic, to criticise in public the physical peculiarities of one's own people, of one's own family, so to speak. Besides, it may be said, and said with justice, that there are plenty of bottled-lightning temperaments in other countries, and plenty of phlegmatic temperaments here; and that, when all is said and done, the more or less of tension about which I am making such a fuss is a very small item in the sum total of a nation's life, and not worth solemn treatment at a time when agreeable rather than disagreeable things should be talked about. Well, in one sense the more or less of tension in our faces and in our unused muscles *is* a small thing: not much mechanical work is done by these contractions. But it is not always the material size of a thing that measures its importance: often it is its place and function. One of the most philosophical remarks I ever heard made was by an unlettered workman who was doing some repairs at my house many years ago. "There is very little difference between one man and another," he said, "when you go to the bottom of it. But what little there is, is very important." And the remark certainly applies to this case. The general over-contraction may be small when estimated in foot-pounds, but its importance is immense on account of its *effects on the over-contracted person's spiritual life*. This follows as a necessary consequence from the theory of our emotions to which I made reference at the beginning of this article. For by the sensations that so incessantly pour in from the over-tense excited body the over-tense and excited habit of mind is kept up; and the sultry, threatening, exhausting, thunderous inner atmosphere never quite clears away. If you never wholly give yourself up to the chair you sit in, but always keep your leg- and body-muscles half contracted for a rise; if you breathe eighteen or nineteen instead of sixteen times a minute, and never quite breathe out at that,—what mental mood *can* you be in but one of inner panting and expectancy, and how can the future and its worries possibly forsake your mind? On the other hand, how can they gain admission to your mind if your brow be unruffled, your respiration calm and complete, and your muscles all relaxed?

Now what is the cause of this absence of repose, this bottled-lightning quality in us Americans? The explanation of it that is usually given is that it comes from the extreme dryness of our climate and the acrobatic performances of our thermometer, coupled with the extraordinary progressiveness of our life, the hard work, the railroad speed, the rapid success, and all the other things we know so well by heart. Well, our climate is certainly exciting, but hardly more so than that of many parts of Europe, where nevertheless no bottled-lightning girls are found. And the work done and the pace of life are as extreme in every great capital of Europe as they are here. To me both of these pretended causes are utterly insufficient to explain the facts.

To explain them, we must go not to physical geography, but to psychology and sociology. The latest chapter both in sociology and in psychology to be developed in a manner that approaches adequacy is the chapter on the imitative impulse. First Bagehot, then Tarde, then Royce and Baldwin here, have shown that invention and imitation, taken together, form, one may say, the entire warp and woof of human life, in so far as it is social. The American over-tension and jerkiness and breathlessness and intensity and agony of expression are primarily social, and only secondarily physiological, phenomena. They are *bad habits*, nothing more or less, bred of custom and example, born of the imitation of bad models and the cultivation of false personal ideals. How are idioms acquired, how do local peculiarities of phrase and accent come about? Through an accidental example set by some one, which struck the ears of others, and was quoted and copied till at last every one in the locality chimed in. Just so it is with national tricks of vocalization or intonation, with national manners, fashions of movement and gesture, and habitual expressions of face. We, here in America, through following a succession of pattern-setters whom it is now impossible to trace, and through influencing each other in a bad direction, have at last settled down collectively into what, for better or worse, is our own characteristic national type,— a type with the production of which, so far as these habits go, the climate and conditions have had practically nothing at all to do.

This type, which we have thus reached by our imitativeness, we now have fixed upon us, for better or worse. Now no type can be *wholly* disadvantageous; but, so far as our type follows the bottled-lightning fashion, it cannot be wholly good. Dr. Clouston was certainly right in thinking that eagerness, breathlessness, and anxiety are not signs of strength: they are signs of weakness and of bad co-ordination. The even forehead, the slab-like cheek, the codfish eye, may be less interesting for the moment; but they are more promising signs than intense expression is of what we may expect of their possessor in the long run. Your dull, unhurried worker gets over a great deal of ground, because he never goes backward or breaks down. Your intense, convulsive worker breaks down and has bad moods so often that you never know where he may be when you most need his help,—he may be having one of his 'bad days.' We say that so many of our fellow-countrymen collapse, and have to be sent abroad to rest their nerves, because they work so hard. I suspect that this is an immense mistake. I suspect that neither the nature nor the amount of our work is accountable for the frequency

and severity of our breakdowns, but that their cause lies
rather in those absurd feelings of hurry and having no
time, in that breathlessness and tension, that anxiety of
feature and that solicitude for results, that lack of inner
harmony and ease, in short, by which with us the work is
so apt to be accompanied, and from which a European
who should do the same work would nine times out of ten
be free. These perfectly wanton and unnecessary tricks of
inner attitude and outer manner in us, caught from the
social atmosphere, kept up by tradition, and idealized by
many as the admirable way of life, are the last straws that
break the American camel's back, the final overflowers of
our measure of wear and tear and fatigue.

The voice, for example, in a surprisingly large number of
us has a tired and plaintive sound. Some of us are really
tired (for I do not mean absolutely to deny that our
climate has a tiring quality); but far more of us are not
tired at all, or would not be tired at all unless we had got
into a wretched trick of feeling tired, by following the
prevalent habits of vocalization and expression. And if
talking high and tired, and living excitedly and hurriedly,
would only enable us to *do* more by the way, even while
breaking us down in the end, it would be different. There
would be some compensation, some excuse, for going on
so. But the exact reverse is the case. It is your relaxed and
easy worker, who is in no hurry, and quite thoughtless most
of the while of consequences, who is your efficient worker;
and tension and anxiety, and present and future, all mixed
up together in our mind at once, are the surest drags upon
steady progress and hindrances to our success. My colleague, Professor Münsterberg, an excellent observer, who
came here recently, has written some notes on America to
German papers. He says in substance that the appearance
of unusual energy in America is superficial and illusory,
being really due to nothing but the habits of jerkiness and
bad co-ordination for which we have to thank the defective
training of our people. I think myself that it is high time
for old legends and traditional opinions to be changed;
and that, if any one should begin to write about Yankee

inefficiency and feebleness, and inability to do anything
with time except to waste it, he would have a very pretty
paradoxical little thesis to sustain, with a great many facts
to quote, and a great deal of experience to appeal to in its
proof.

Well, my friends, if our dear American character is
weakened by all this over-tension,—and I think, whatever
reserves you may make, that you will agree as to the main
facts,—where does the remedy lie? It lies, of course, where
lay the origins of the disease. If a vicious fashion and
taste are to blame for the thing, the fashion and taste must
be changed. And, though it is no small thing to inoculate
seventy millions of people with new standards, yet, if there
is to be any relief, that will have to be done. We must
change ourselves from a race that admires jerk and snap
for their own sakes, and looks down upon low voices and
quiet ways as dull, to one that, on the contrary, has calm
for its ideal, and for their own sakes loves harmony, dignity, and ease.

So we go back to the psychology of imitation again.
There is only one way to improve ourselves, and that is by
some of us setting an example which the others may pick
up and imitate till the new fashion spreads from east to
west. Some of us are in more favorable positions than
others to set new fashions. Some are much more striking
personally and imitable, so to speak. But no living person
is sunk so low as not to be imitated by somebody. Thack-
eray somewhere says of the Irish nation that there never
was an Irishman so poor that he didn't have a still poorer
Irishman living at his expense; and, surely, there is no
human being whose example doesn't work contagiously in
some particular. The very idiots at our public institutions
imitate each other's peculiarities. And, if you should individually achieve calmness and harmony in your own person, you may depend upon it that a wave of imitation will
spread from you, as surely as the circles spread outward
when a stone is dropped into a lake.

Fortunately, we shall not have to be absolute pioneers.
Even now in New York they have formed a society for the

improvement of our national vocalization, and one perceives its machinations already in the shape of various newspaper paragraphs intended to stir up dissatisfaction with the awful thing that it is. And, better still than that, because more radical and general, is the gospel of relaxation, as one may call it, preached by Miss Annie Payson Call, of Boston, in her admirable little volume called 'Power through Repose,' a book that ought to be in the hands of every teacher and student in America of either sex. You need only be followers, then, on a path already opened up by others. But of one thing be confident: others still will follow you.

And this brings me to one more application of psychology to practical life, to which I will call attention briefly, and then close. If one's example of easy and calm ways is to be effectively contagious, one feels by instinct that the less voluntarily one aims at getting imitated, the more unconscious one keeps in the matter, the more likely one is to succeed. *Become the imitable thing,* and you may then discharge your minds of all responsibility for the imitation. The laws of social nature will take care of that result. Now the psychological principle on which this precept reposes is a law of very deep and wide-spread importance in the conduct of our lives, and at the same time a law which we Americans most grievously neglect. Stated technically, the law is this: that *strong feeling about one's self tends to arrest the free association of one's objective ideas and motor processes.* We get the extreme example of this in the mental disease called melancholia.

A melancholic patient is filled through and through with intensely painful emotion about himself. He is threatened, he is guilty, he is doomed, he is annihilated, he is lost. His mind is fixed as if in a cramp on these feelings of his own situation, and in all the books on insanity you may read that the usual varied flow of his thoughts has ceased. His associative processes, to use the technical phrase, are inhibited; and his ideas stand stock-still, shut up to their one monotonous function of reiterating inwardly the fact of the man's desperate estate. And this inhibitive influence is not due to the mere fact that his emotion is *painful.* Joyous emotions about the self also stop the association of our ideas. A saint in ecstasy is as motionless and irresponsive and one-idea'd as a melancholiac. And, without going as far as ecstatic saints, we know how in every one a great or sudden pleasure may paralyze the flow of thought. Ask young people returning from a party or a spectacle, and all excited about it, what it was. "Oh, it was *fine!* it was *fine!* it was *fine!*" is all the information you are likely to receive until the excitement has calmed down. Probably every one of my hearers has been made temporarily half-idiotic by some great success or piece of good fortune. "*Good!* GOOD! GOOD!" is all we can at such times say to ourselves until we smile at our own very foolishness.

Now from all this we can draw an extremely practical conclusion. If, namely, we wish our trains of ideation and volition to be copious and varied and effective, we must form the habit of freeing them from the inhibitive influence of reflection upon them, of egoistic preoccupation about their results. Such a habit, like other habits, can be formed. Prudence and duty and self-regard, emotions of ambition and emotions of anxiety, have, of course, a needful part to play in our lives. But confine them as far as possible to the occasions when you are making your general resolutions and deciding on your plans of campaign, and keep them out of the details. When once a decision is reached and execution is the order of the day, dismiss absolutely all responsibility and care about the outcome. *Unclamp,* in a word, your intellectual and practical machinery, and let it run free; and the service it will do you will be twice as good. Who are the scholars who get 'rattled' in the recitation-room? Those who think of the possibilities of failure and feel the great importance of the act. Who are those who do recite well? Often those who are most indifferent. *Their* ideas reel themselves out of their memory of their own accord. Why do we hear the complaint so often that social life in New England is either less rich and expressive or more fatiguing than it is

in some other parts of the world? To what is the fact, if
fact it be, due unless to the over-active conscience of the
people, afraid of either saying something too trivial and
obvious, or something insincere, or something unworthy of
one's interlocutor, or something in some way or other not
adequate to the occasion? How can conversation possibly
steer itself through such a sea of responsibilities and inhibitions as this? On the other hand, conversation does
flourish and society is refreshing, and neither dull on the
one hand nor exhausting from its effort on the other,
wherever people forget their scruples and take the brakes
off their hearts, and let their tongues wag as automatically
and irresponsibly as they will.

They talk much in pedagogic circles to-day about the
duty of the teacher to prepare for every lesson in advance.
To some extent this is useful. But we Yankees are assuredly not those to whom such a general doctrine should
be preached. We are only too careful as it is. The advice I
should give to most teachers would be in the words of
one who is herself an admirable teacher. Prepare yourself in
the *subject so well that it shall be always on tap*: then in
the class-room trust your spontaneity and fling away all
further care.

My advice to students, especially to girl-students, would
be somewhat similar. Just as a bicycle-chain may be too
tight, so may one's carefulness and conscientiousness be
so tense as to hinder the running of one's mind. Take, for
example, periods when there are many successive days of
examination impending. One ounce of good nervous tone
in an examination is worth many pounds of anxious study
for it in advance. If you want really to do your best in
an examination, fling away the book the day before, say
to yourself, "I won't waste another minute on this miserable thing, and I don't care an iota whether I succeed or
not." Say this sincerely, and feel it; and go out and play, or
go to bed and sleep, and I am sure the results next day will
encourage you to use the method permanently. I have
heard this advice given to a student by Miss Call, whose
book on muscular relaxation I quoted a moment ago. In

her later book, entitled 'As a Matter of Course,' the gospel of moral relaxation, of dropping things from the mind, and not 'caring,' is preached with equal success. Not only our preachers, but our friends the theosophists and mind-curers of various religious sects are also harping on this string. And with the doctors, the Delsarteans, the various mind-curing sects, and such writers as Mr. Dresser, Prentice Mulford, Mr. Horace Fletcher, and Mr. Trine to help, and the whole band of schoolteachers and magazine-readers chiming in, it really looks as if a good start might be made in the direction of changing our American mental habit into something more indifferent and strong.

Worry means always and invariably inhibition of associations and loss of effective power. Of course, the sovereign cure for worry is religious faith; and this, of course, you also know. The turbulent billows of the fretful surface leave the deep parts of the ocean undisturbed, and to him who has a hold on vaster and more permanent realities the hourly vicissitudes of his personal destiny seem relatively insignificant things. The really religious person is accordingly unshakable and full of equanimity, and calmly ready for any duty that the day may bring forth. This is charmingly illustrated by a little work with which I recently became acquainted, "The Practice of the Presence of God, the Best Ruler of a Holy Life, by Brother Lawrence, being Conversations and Letters of Nicholas Herman of Lorraine, Translated from the French." * I extract a few passages, the conversations being given in indirect discourse. Brother Lawrence was a Carmelite friar, converted at Paris in 1666. "He said that he had been footman to M. Fieubert, the Treasurer, and that he was a great awkward fellow, who broke everything. That he had desired to be received into a monastery, thinking that he would there be made to smart for his awkwardness and the faults he should commit, and so he should sacrifice to God his life, with its pleasures; but that God had disappointed him, he having met with nothing but satisfaction in that state. . . .

* Fleming H. Revell Company, New York.

"That he had long been troubled in mind from a certain belief that he should be damned; that all the men in the world could not have persuaded him to the contrary; but that he had thus reasoned with himself about it: *I engaged in a religious life only for the love of God, and I have endeavored to act only for Him; whatever becomes of me, whether I be lost or saved, I will always continue to act purely for the love of God. I shall have this good at least, that till death I shall have done all that is in me to love Him.* . . . That since then he had passed his life in perfect liberty and continual joy.

"That when an occasion of practising some virtue offered, he addressed himself to God, saying, 'Lord, I cannot do this unless thou enablest me'; and that then he received strength more than sufficient. That, when he had failed in his duty, he only confessed his fault, saying to God, 'I shall never do otherwise, if You leave me to myself; it is You who must hinder my failing, and mend what is amiss.' That after this he gave himself no further uneasiness about it.

"That he had been lately sent into Burgundy to buy the provision of wine for the society, which was a very unwelcome task for him, because he had no turn for business, and because he was lame, and could not go about the boat but by rolling himself over the casks. That, however, he gave himself no uneasiness about it, nor about the purchase of the wine. That he said to God, 'It was his business he was about,' and that he afterward found it well performed. That he had been sent into Auvergne, the year before, upon the same account; that he could not tell how the matter passed, but that it proved very well.

"So, likewise, in his business in the kitchen (to which he had naturally a great aversion), having accustomed himself to do everything there for the love of God, and with prayer upon all occasions, for his grace to do his work well, he had found everything easy during fifteen years that he had been employed there.

"That he was very well pleased with the post he was now in, but that he was as ready to quit that as the former, since he was always pleasing himself in every condition, by doing little things for the love of God.

"That the goodness of God assured him he would not forsake him utterly, and that he would give him strength to bear whatever evil he permitted to happen to him; and, therefore, that he feared nothing, and had no occasion to consult with anybody about his state. That, when he had attempted to do it, he had always come away more perplexed."

The simple-heartedness of the good Brother Lawrence, and the relaxation of all unnecessary solicitudes and anxieties in him, is a refreshing spectacle.

The need of feeling responsible all the livelong day has been preached long enough in our New England. Long enough exclusively, at any rate,—and long enough to the female sex. What our girl-students and woman-teachers most need nowadays is not the exacerbation, but rather the toning-down of their moral tensions. Even now I fear that some one of my fair hearers may be making an undying resolve to become strenuously relaxed, cost what it will, for the remainder of her life. It is needless to say that that is not the way to do it. The way to do it, paradoxical as it may seem, is genuinely not to care whether you are doing it or not. Then, possibly, by the grace of God, you may all at once find that you *are* doing it, and, having learned what the trick feels like, you may (again by the grace of God) be enabled to go on.

And that something like this may be the happy experience of all my hearers is, in closing, my most earnest wish.

CHAPTER 2

On a Certain Blindness in Human Beings

Our judgments concerning the worth of things, big or little, depend on the *feelings* the things arouse in us. Where we judge a thing to be precious in consequence of the *idea* we frame of it, this is only because the idea is itself associated already with a feeling. If we were radically feelingless, and if ideas were the only things our mind could entertain, we should lose all our likes and dislikes at a stroke, and be unable to point to any one situation or experience in life more valuable or significant than any other.

Now the blindness in human beings, of which this discourse will treat, is the blindness with which we all are afflicted in regard to the feelings of creatures and people different from ourselves.

We are practical beings, each of us with limited functions and duties to perform. Each is bound to feel intensely the importance of his own duties and the significance of the situations that call these forth. But this feeling is in each of us a vital secret, for sympathy with which we vainly look to others. The others are too much absorbed in their own vital secrets to take an interest in ours. Hence the stupidity and injustice of our opinions, so far as they deal with the significance of alien lives. Hence the falsity of our judgments, so far as they presume to decide in an absolute way on the value of other persons' conditions or ideals.

Take our dogs and ourselves, connected as we are by a tie more intimate than most ties in this world; and yet, outside of that tie of friendly fondness, how insensible, each of us, to all that makes life significant for the other! —we to the rapture of bones under hedges, or smells of trees and lamp-posts, they to the delights of literature and art. As you sit reading the most moving romance you ever fell upon, what sort of a judge is your fox-terrier of your behavior? With all his good will toward you, the nature of your conduct is absolutely excluded from his comprehension. To sit there like a senseless statue, when you might be taking him to walk and throwing sticks for him to catch! What queer disease is this that comes over you every day, of holding things and staring at them like that for hours together, paralyzed of motion and vacant of all conscious life? The African savages came nearer the truth; but they, too, missed it, when they gathered wonderingly round one of our American travellers who, in the interior, had just come into possession of a stray copy of the New York *Commercial Advertiser*, and was devouring it column by column. When he got through, they offered him a high price for the mysterious object; and, being asked for what they wanted it, they said: "For an eye medicine,"—that being the only reason they could conceive of for the protracted bath which he had given his eyes upon its surface.

The spectator's judgment is sure to miss the root of the matter, and to possess no truth. The subject judged knows a part of the world of reality which the judging spectator fails to see, knows more while the spectator knows less; and, wherever there is conflict of opinion and difference of vision, we are bound to believe that the truer side is the side that feels the more, and not the side that feels the less.

Let me take a personal example of the kind that befalls each one of us daily:—

Some years ago, while journeying in the mountains of North Carolina, I passed by a large number of 'coves,' as they call them there, or heads of small valleys between the hills, which had been newly cleared and planted. The impression on my mind was one of unmitigated squalor. The settler had in every case cut down the more manageable trees, and left their charred stumps standing. The larger trees he had girdled and killed, in order that their foliage should not cast a shade. He had then built a log cabin, plastering its chinks with clay, and had set up a tall zigzag rail fence around the scene of his havoc, to keep the pigs and cattle out. Finally, he had irregularly planted the intervals between the stumps and trees with Indian corn, which grew among the chips; and there he dwelt with his wife and babes—an axe, a gun, a few utensils, and some pigs and chickens feeding in the woods, being the sum total of his possessions.

The forest had been destroyed; and what had 'improved' it out of existence was hideous, a sort of ulcer, without a single element of artificial grace to make up for the loss of Nature's beauty. Ugly, indeed, seemed the life of the squatter, scudding, as the sailors say, under bare poles, beginning again away back where our first ancestors started, and by hardly a single item the better off for all the achievements of the intervening generations.

Talk about going back to nature! I said to myself, oppressed by the dreariness, as I drove by. Talk of a country life for one's old age and for one's children! Never thus, with nothing but the bare ground and one's bare hands to fight the battle! Never, without the best spoils of culture woven in! The beauties and commodities gained by the centuries are sacred. They are our heritage and birthright. No modern person ought to be willing to live a day in such a state of rudimentariness and denudation.

Then I said to the mountaineer who was driving me, "What sort of people are they who have to make these new clearings?" "All of us," he replied. "Why, we ain't happy here, unless we are getting one of these coves under cultivation." I instantly felt that I had been losing the whole inward significance of the situation. Because to me the clearings spoke of naught but denudation, I thought that to those whose sturdy arms and obedient axes had made them they could tell no other story. But, when *they* looked on the hideous stumps, what they thought of was personal victory. The chips, the girdled trees, and the vile split rails spoke of honest sweat, persistent toil and final reward. The cabin was a warrant of safety for self and wife and babes. In short, the clearing, which to me was a mere ugly picture on the retina, was to them a symbol redolent with moral memories and sang a very pæan of duty, struggle, and success.

I had been as blind to the peculiar ideality of their conditions as they certainly would also have been to the ideality of mine, had they had a peep at my strange indoor academic ways of life at Cambridge.

Wherever a process of life communicates an eagerness to him who lives it, there the life becomes genuinely significant. Sometimes the eagerness is more knit up with the motor activities, sometimes with the perceptions, sometimes with the imagination, sometimes with reflective thought. But, wherever it is found, there is the zest, the tingle, the excitement of reality; and there *is* 'importance' in the only real and positive sense in which importance ever anywhere can be.

Robert Louis Stevenson has illustrated this by a case, drawn from the sphere of the imagination, in an essay which I really think deserves to become immortal, both for the truth of its matter and the excellence of its form.

"Toward the end of September," Stevenson writes, "when school-time was drawing near, and the nights were already black, we would begin to sally from our respective villas, each equipped with a tin bull's-eye lantern. The thing was so well known that it had worn a rut in the commerce of Great Britain; and the grocers, about the due time, began to garnish their windows with our particular brand of luminary. We wore them buckled to the waist upon a cricket belt, and over them, such was the rigor of the game, a buttoned top-coat. They smelled noisomely of blistered tin. They never burned aright, though they would always burn our fingers. Their use was naught, the pleasure of them merely fanciful, and yet a boy with a bull's-eye under his top-coat asked for nothing more. The fishermen

used lanterns about their boats, and it was from them, I
suppose, that we had got the hint; but theirs were not
bull's-eyes, nor did we ever play at being fishermen. The
police carried them at their belts, and we had plainly
copied them in that; yet we did not pretend to be policemen. Burglars, indeed, we may have had some haunting
thought of; and we had certainly an eye to past ages when
lanterns were more common, and to certain story-books
in which we had found them to figure very largely. But
take it for all in all, the pleasure of the thing was sub-
stantive; and to be a boy with a bull's-eye under his top-
coat was good enough for us.

"When two of these asses met, there would be an anxious 'Have you got your lantern?' and a gratified 'Yes!'
That was the shibboleth, and very needful, too; for, as it
was the rule to keep our glory contained, none could recognize a lantern-bearer unless (like the polecat) by the
smell. Four or five would sometimes climb into the belly
of a ten-man lugger, with nothing but the thwarts above
them,—for the cabin was usually locked,—or choose out
some hollow of the links where the wind might whistle
overhead. Then the coats would be unbuttoned, and the
bull's-eyes discovered; and in the chequering glimmer,
under the huge, windy hall of the night, and cheered by
a rich steam of toasting tinware, these fortunate young
gentlemen would crouch together in the cold sand of the
links, or on the scaly bilges of the fishing-boat, and delight
them with inappropriate talk. Woe is me that I cannot
give some specimens! . . . But the talk was but a condi-
ment, and these gatherings themselves only accidents in
the career of the lantern-bearer. The essence of this bliss
was to walk by yourself in the black night, the slide shut,
the top-coat buttoned, not a ray escaping, whether to conduct your footsteps or to make your glory public,—a mere
pillar of darkness in the dark; and all the while, deep down
in the privacy of your fool's heart, to know you had a
bull's-eye at your belt, and to exult and sing over the
knowledge.

"It is said that a poet has died young in the breast of

the most stolid. It may be contended rather that a (somewhat minor) bard in almost every case survives, and is the
spice of life to his possessor. Justice is not done to the
versatility and the unplumbed childishness of man's imagination. His life from without may seem but a rude mound
of mud: there will be some golden chamber at the heart
of it, in which he dwells delighted; and for as dark as his
pathway seems to the observer, he will have some kind of
bull's-eye at his belt.

. . . "There is one fable that touches very near the
quick of life,—the fable of the monk who passed into the
woods, heard a bird break into song, hearkened for a trill
or two, and found himself at his return a stranger at his
convent gates; for he had been absent fifty years, and of
all his comrades there survived but one to recognize him.
It is not only in the woods that this enchanter carols,
though perhaps he is native there. He sings in the most
doleful places. The miser hears him and chuckles, and his
days are moments. With no more apparatus than an evil-
smelling lantern, I have evoked him on the naked links.
All life that is not merely mechanical is spun out of two
strands,—seeking for that bird and hearing him. And it is
just this that makes life so hard to value, and the delight
of each so incommunicable. And it is just a knowledge of
this, and a remembrance of those fortunate hours in which
the bird *has* sung to *us*, that fills us with such wonder when
we turn to the pages of the realist. There, to be sure, we
find a picture of life in so far as it consists of mud and of
old iron, cheap desires and cheap fears, that which we are
ashamed to remember and that which we are careless
whether we forget; but of the note of that time-devouring
nightingale we hear no news.

. . . "Say that we came [in such a realistic romance]
on some such business as that of my lantern-bearers on the
links, and described the boys as very cold, spat upon by
flurries of rain, and drearily surrounded, all of which they
were; and their talk as silly and indecent, which it certainly was. To the eye of the observer they *are* wet and
cold and drearily surrounded; but ask themselves, and they

are in the heaven of a recondite pleasure, the ground of which is an ill-smelling lantern.

"For, to repeat, the ground of a man's joy is often hard to hit. It may hinge at times upon a mere accessory, like the lantern; it may reside in the mysterious inwards of psychology. . . . It has so little bond with externals . . . that it may even touch them not, and the man's true life, for which he consents to live, lie together in the field of fancy. . . . In such a case the poetry runs underground. The observer (poor soul, with his documents!) is all abroad. For to look at the man is but to court deception. We shall see the trunk from which he draws his nourishment; but he himself is above and abroad in the green dome of foliage, hummed through by winds and nested in by nightingales. And the true realism were that of the poets, to climb after him like a squirrel, and catch some glimpse of the heaven in which he lives. And the true realism, always and everywhere, is that of the poets: to find out where joy resides, and give it a voice far beyond singing.

"For to miss the joy is to miss all. In the joy of the actors lies the sense of any action. That is the explanation, that the excuse. To one who has not the secret of the lanterns the scene upon the links is meaningless. And hence the haunting and truly spectral unreality of realistic books. . . . In each we miss the personal poetry, the enchanted atmosphere, that rainbow work of fancy that clothes what is naked and seems to ennoble what is base; in each, life falls dead like dough, instead of soaring away like a balloon into the colors of the sunset; each is true, each inconceivable; for no man lives in the external truth among salts and acids, but in the warm, phantasmagoric chamber of his brain, with the painted windows and the storied wall." *

These paragraphs are the best thing I know in all Stevenson. "To miss the joy is to miss all." Indeed, it is. Yet we are but finite, and each one of us has some single

* 'The Lantern-bearers,' in the volume entitled 'Across the Plains.' Abridged in the quotation.

specialized vocation of his own. And it seems as if energy in the service of its particular duties might be got only by hardening the heart toward everything unlike them. Our deadness toward all but one particular kind of joy would thus be the price we inevitably have to pay for being practical creatures. Only in some pitiful dreamer, some philosopher, poet, or romancer, or when the common practical man becomes a lover, does the hard externality give way, and a gleam of insight into the ejective world, as Clifford called it, the vast world of inner life beyond us, so different from that of outer seeming, illuminate our mind. Then the whole scheme of our customary values gets confounded, then our self is riven and its narrow interests fly to pieces, then a new centre and a new perspective must be found.

The change is well described by my colleague, Josiah Royce:—

"What, then, is our neighbor? Thou hast regarded his thought, his feeling, as somehow different from thine. Thou hast said, 'A pain in him is not like a pain in me, but something far easier to bear.' He seems to thee a little less living than thou; his life is dim, it is cold, it is a pale fire beside thy own burning desires. . . . So, dimly and by instinct hast thou lived with thy neighbor, and hast known him not, being blind. Thou hast made [of him] a thing, no Self at all. Have done with this illusion, and simply try to learn the truth. Pain is pain, joy is joy, everywhere, even as in thee. In all the songs of the forest birds; in all the cries of the wounded and dying, struggling in the captor's power; in the boundless sea where the myriads of water-creatures strive and die; amid all the countless hordes of savage men; in all sickness and sorrow; in all exultation and hope, everywhere, from the lowest to the noblest, the same conscious, burning, wilful life is found, endlessly manifold as the forms of the living creatures, unquenchable as the fires of the sun, real as these impulses that even now throb in thine own little selfish heart. Lift up thy eyes, behold that life, and then turn away, and forget it as thou canst; but, if thou hast *known* that, thou hast begun to know thy duty." *

This higher vision of an inner significance in what, until then, we had realized only in the dead external way, often comes over a person suddenly; and, when it does so, it makes an epoch in his history. As Emerson says, there is a depth in those moments that constrains us to ascribe more reality to them than to all other experiences. The passion of love will shake one like an explosion, or some act will awaken a remorseful compunction that hangs like a cloud over all one's later day.

This mystic sense of hidden meaning starts upon us often from non-human natural things. I take this passage from 'Obermann,' a French novel that had some vogue in its day: "Paris, March 7.—It was dark and rather cold. I was gloomy, and walked because I had nothing to do. I passed by some flowers placed breast-high upon a wall. A jonquil in bloom was there. It is the strongest expression of desire: it was the first perfume of the year. I felt all the happiness destined for man. This unutterable harmony of souls, the phantom of the ideal world, arose in me complete. I never felt anything so great or so instantaneous. I know not what shape, what analogy, what secret of relation it was that made me see in this flower a limitless beauty. . . . I shall never enclose in a conception this power, this immensity that nothing will express; this form that nothing will contain; this ideal of a better world which one feels, but which it would seem that nature has not made." †

Wordsworth and Shelley are similarly full of this sense of a limitless significance in natural things. In Wordsworth it was a somewhat austere and moral significance,— a 'lonely cheer.'

> "To every natural form, rock, fruit, or flower,
> Even the loose stones that cover the highway,

* The Religious Aspect of Philosophy, pp. 157-162 (abridged).
† De Sénancour: Obermann, Lettre XXX.

I gave a moral life: I saw them feel
Or linked them to some feeling: the great mass
Lay bedded in some quickening soul, and all
That I beheld respired with inward meaning." *

"Authentic tidings of invisible things!" Just what this
hidden presence in nature was, which Wordsworth so
rapturously felt, and in the light of which he lived, tramping the hills for days together, the poet never could explain logically or in articulate conceptions. Yet to the
reader who may himself have had gleaming moments of
a similar sort the verses in which Wordsworth simply pro-
claims the fact of them come with a heart-satisfying au-
thority:—

"Magnificent
The morning rose, in memorable pomp,
Glorious as e'er I had beheld. In front
The sea lay laughing at a distance; near

The solid mountains shone, bright as the clouds,
Grain-tinctured, drenched in empyrean light;
And in the meadows and the lower grounds
Was all the sweetness of a common dawn,—
Dews, vapors, and the melody of birds,
And laborers going forth to till the fields.

"Ah! need I say, dear Friend, that to the brim
My heart was full; I made no vows, but vows
Were then made for me; bond unknown to me
Was given, that I should be, else sinning greatly,
A dedicated Spirit. On I walked,
In thankful blessedness, which yet survives." †

As Wordsworth walked, filled with his strange inner
joy, responsive thus to the secret life of nature round about
him, his rural neighbors, tightly and narrowly intent upon
their own affairs, their crops and lambs and fences, must
have thought him a very insignificant and foolish personage.
It surely never occurred to any one of them to wonder what
was going on inside of *him* or what it might be worth.
And yet that inner life of his carried the burden of a sig-

* The Prelude, Book III.
† The Prelude, Book IV.

nificance that has fed the souls of others, and fills them to this day with inner joy.

Richard Jefferies has written a remarkable autobiographic document entitled The Story of my Heart. It tells, in many pages, of the rapture with which in youth the sense of the life of nature filled him. On a certain hill-top he says:—

"I was utterly alone with the sun and the earth. Lying down on the grass, I spoke in my soul to the earth, the sun, the air, and the distant sea, far beyond sight. . . . With all the intensity of feeling which exalted me, all the intense communion I held with the earth, the sun and sky, the stars hidden by the light, with the ocean,—in no manner can the thrilling depth of these feelings be written,— with these I prayed as if they were the keys of an instrument. . . . The great sun, burning with light, the strong earth,—dear earth,—the warm sky, the pure air, the thought of ocean, the inexpressible beauty of all filled me with a rapture, an ecstasy, an inflatus. With this inflatus, too, I prayed. . . . The prayer, this soul-emotion, was in itself, not for an object: it was a passion. I hid my face in the grass. I was wholly prostrated, I lost myself in the wrestle, I was rapt and carried away. . . . Had any shepherd accidentally seen me lying on the turf, he would only have thought I was resting a few minutes. I made no outward show. Who could have imagined the whirlwind of passion that was going on in me as I reclined there!" *

Surely, a worthless hour of life, when measured by the usual standards of commercial value. Yet in what other *kind* of value can the preciousness of any hour, made precious by any standard, consist, if it consist not in feelings of excited significance like these, engendered in some one, by what the hour contains?

Yet so blind and dead does the clamor of our own practical interests make us to all other things, that it seems almost as if it were necessary to become worthless as a practical being, if one is to hope to attain to any breadth of insight into the impersonal world of worths as such,

* *Op. cit.*, Boston, Roberts, 1883, pp. 5, 6.

to have any perception of life's meaning on a large objective scale. Only your mystic, your dreamer, or your insolvent tramp or loafer, can afford so sympathetic an occupation, an occupation which will change the usual standards of human value in the twinkling of an eye, giving to foolishness a place ahead of power, and laying low in a minute the distinctions which it takes a hard-working conventional man a lifetime to build up. You may be a prophet, at this rate; but you cannot be a worldly success.

Walt Whitman, for instance, is accounted by many of us a contemporary prophet. He abolishes the usual human distinctions, brings all conventionalisms into solution, and loves and celebrates hardly any human attributes save those elementary ones common to all members of the race. For this he becomes a sort of ideal tramp, a rider on omnibus-tops and ferry-boats, and, considered either practically or academically, a worthless, unproductive being. His verses are but ejaculations—things mostly without subject or verb, a succession of interjections on an immense scale. He felt the human crowd as rapturously as Wordsworth felt the mountains, felt it as an overpoweringly significant presence, simply to absorb one's mind in which should be business sufficient and worthy to fill the days of a serious man. As he crosses Brooklyn ferry, this is what he feels:—

Flood-tide below me! I watch you, face to face;
Clouds of the west! sun there half an hour high! I see you also
    face to face.
Crowds of men and women attired in the usual costumes! how
    curious you are to me!
On the ferry-boats, the hundreds and hundreds that cross, return-
    ing home, are more curious to me than you suppose;
And you that shall cross from shore to shore years hence, are
    more to me, and more in my meditations, than you might
    suppose.
Others will enter the gates of the ferry, and cross from shore to
    shore;
Others will watch the run of the flood-tide;
Others will see the shipping of Manhattan north and west, and
    the heights of Brooklyn to the south and east;
Others will see the islands large and small;

Fifty years hence, others will see them as they cross, the sun half
    an hour high.
A hundred years hence, or ever so many hundred years hence,
    others will see them,
Will enjoy the sunset, the pouring in of the flood-tide, the falling
    back to the sea of the ebb-tide.
It avails not, neither time or place—distance avails not.
Just as you feel when you look on the river and sky, so I felt;
Just as any of you is one of a living crowd, I was one of a crowd;
Just as you are refresh'd by the gladness of the river and the
    bright flow, I was refresh'd;
Just as you stand and lean on the rail, yet hurry with the swift
    current, I stood, yet was hurried;
Just as you look on the numberless masts of ships, and the thick-
    stemmed pipes of steamboats, I looked.
I too many and many a time cross'd the river, the sun half an
    hour high;
I watched the Twelfth-month sea-gulls—I saw them high in the
    air, with motionless wings, oscillating their bodies,
I saw how the glistening yellow lit up parts of their bodies, and
    left the rest in strong shadow,
I saw the slow-wheeling circles, and the gradual edging toward
    the south.
Saw the white sails of schooners and sloops, saw the ships at
    anchor,
The sailors at work in the rigging, or out astride the spars;
The scallop-edged waves in the twilight, the ladled cups, the
    frolicsome crests and glistening;
The stretch afar growing dimmer and dimmer, the gray walls of
    the granite store-houses by the docks;
On the neighboring shores, the fires from the foundry chimneys
    burning high . . . . into the night,
Casting their flicker of black . . . . into the clefts of streets.
These, and all else, were to me the same as they are to you.*

And so on, through the rest of a divinely beautiful
poem. And, if you wish to see what this hoary loafer considered the most worthy way of profiting by life's heaven-
sent opportunities, read the delicious volume of his letters
to a young car-conductor who had become his friend:—

"NEW YORK, Oct. 9, 1868.

"*Dear Pete,*—It is splendid here this forenoon—
bright and cool. I was out early taking a short walk by the

* 'Crossing Brooklyn Ferry' (abridged).

river only two squares from where I live. . . . Shall I tell you about [my life] just to fill up? I generally spend the forenoon in my room writing, etc., then take a bath fix up and go out about twelve and loafe somewhere or call on someone down town or on business, or perhaps if it is very pleasant and I feel like it ride a trip with some driver friend on Broadway from 23rd Street to Bowling Green, three miles each way. (Every day I find I have plenty to do, every hour is occupied with something.) You know it is a never ending amusement and study and recreation for me to ride a couple of hours on a pleasant afternoon on a Broadway stage in this way. You see everything as you pass, a sort of living, endless panorama—shops and splendid buildings and great windows: on the broad sidewalks crowds of women richly dressed continually passing, altogether different, superior in style and looks from any to be seen anywhere else—in fact a perfect stream of people—men too dressed in high style, and plenty of foreigners—and then in the streets the thick crowd of carriages, stages, carts, hotel and private coaches, and in fact all sorts of vehicles and many first class teams, mile after mile, and the splendor of such a great street and so many tall, ornamental, noble buildings many of them of white marble, and the gayety and motion on every side: you will not wonder how much attraction all this is on a fine day, to a great loafer like me, who enjoys so much seeing the busy world move by him, and exhibiting itself for his amusement, while he takes it easy and just looks on and observes." *

Truly a futile way of passing the time, some of you may say, and not altogether creditable to a grown-up man. And yet, from the deepest point of view, who knows the more of truth, and who knows the less,—Whitman on his omnibus-top, full of the inner joy with which the spectacle inspires him, or you, full of the disdain which the futility of his occupation excites?

When your ordinary Brooklynite or New Yorker, leading a life replete with too much luxury, or tired and careworn

* Calamus, Boston, 1897, pp. 41, 42.

about his personal affairs, crosses the ferry or goes up Broadway, *his* fancy does not thus 'soar away into the colors of the sunset' as did Whitman's, nor does he inwardly realize at all the indisputable fact that this world never did anywhere or at any time contain more of essential divinity, or of eternal meaning, than is embodied in the fields of vision over which his eyes so carelessly pass. There is life; and there, a step away, is death. There is the only kind of beauty there ever was. There is the old human struggle and its fruits together. There is the text and the sermon, the real and the ideal in one. But to the jaded and unquickened eye it is all dead and common, pure vulgarism, flatness, and disgust. "Hech! it is a sad sight!" says Carlyle, walking at night with some one who appeals to him to note the splendor of the stars. And that very repetition of the scene to new generations of men in *secula seculorum*, that eternal recurrence of the common order, which so fills a Whitman with mystic satisfaction, is to a Schopenhauer, with the emotional anæsthesia, the feeling of 'awful inner emptiness' from out of which he views it all, the chief ingredient of the tedium it instils. What is life on the largest scale, he asks, but the same recurrent inanities, the same dog barking, the same fly buzzing, forevermore? Yet of the kind of fibre of which such inanities consist is the material woven of all the excitements, joys, and meanings that ever were, or ever shall be, in this world.

To be rapt with satisfied attention, like Whitman, to the mere spectacle of the world's presence, is one way, and the most fundamental way, of confessing one's sense of its unfathomable significance and importance. But how can one attain to the feeling of the vital significance of an experience, if one have it not to begin with? There is no receipt which one can follow. Being a secret and a mystery, it often comes in mysteriously unexpected ways. It blossoms sometimes from out of the very grave wherein we imagined that our happiness was buried. Benvenuto Cellini, after a life all in the outer sunshine, made of adventures and artistic excitements, suddenly finds himself cast into a dungeon in the Castle of San Angelo. The place is horrible. Rats and wet and mould possess it. His leg is broken and his teeth fall out, apparently with scurvy. But his thoughts turn to God as they have never turned before. He gets a Bible, which he reads during the one hour in the twenty-four in which a wandering ray of daylight penetrates his cavern. He has religious visions. He sings psalms to himself, and composes hymns. And thinking, on the last day of July, of the festivities customary on the morrow in Rome, he says to himself: "All these past years I celebrated this holiday with the vanities of the world: from this year henceforward I will do it with the divinity of God. And then I said to myself, 'Oh, how much more happy I am for this present life of mine than for all those things remembered!' "*

But the great understander of these mysterious ebbs and flows is Tolstoï. They throb all through his novels. In his 'War and Peace,' the hero, Peter, is supposed to be the richest man in the Russian empire. During the French invasion he is taken prisoner, and dragged through much of the retreat. Cold, vermin, hunger, and every form of misery assail him, the result being a revelation to him of the real scale of life's values. "Here only, and for the first time, he appreciated, because he was deprived of it, the happiness of eating when he was hungry, of drinking when he was thirsty, of sleeping when he was sleepy, and of talking when he felt the desire to exchange some words. . . . Later in life he always recurred with joy to this month of captivity, and never failed to speak with enthusiasm of the powerful and ineffaceable sensations, and especially of the moral calm which he had experienced at this epoch. When at daybreak, on the morrow of his imprisonment, he saw [I abridge here Tolstoï's description] the mountains with their wooded slopes disappearing in the grayish mist; when he felt the cool breeze caress him; when he saw the light drive away the vapors, and the sun rise majestically behind the clouds and cupolas, and the crosses, the dew, the distance, the river, sparkle in the

* Vita, lib. 2, chap. iv.

splendid, cheerful rays,—his heart overflowed with emotion. This emotion kept continually with him, and increased a hundred-fold as the difficulties of his situation grew graver. . . . He learnt that man is meant for happiness, and that this happiness is in him, in the satisfaction of the daily needs of existence, and that unhappiness is the fatal result, not of our need, but of our abundance. . . . When calm reigned in the camp, and the embers paled, and little by little went out, the full moon had reached the zenith. The woods and the fields roundabout lay clearly visible; and, beyond the inundation of light which filled them, the view plunged into the limitless horizon. Then Peter cast his eyes upon the firmament, filled at that hour with myriads of stars. 'All that is mine,' he thought. 'All that is in me, is me! And that is what they think they have taken prisoner! That is what they have shut up in a cabin!' So he smiled, and turned in to sleep among his comrades."*

The occasion and the experience, then, are nothing. It all depends on the capacity of the soul to be grasped, to have its life-currents absorbed by what is given. "Crossing a bare common," says Emerson, "in snow puddles, at twilight, under a clouded sky, without having in my thoughts any occurrence of special good fortune, I have enjoyed a perfect exhilaration. I am glad to the brink of fear."

Life is always worth living, if one have such responsive sensibilities. But we of the highly educated classes (so called) have most of us got far, far away from Nature. We are trained to seek the choice, the rare, the exquisite exclusively, and to overlook the common. We are stuffed with abstract conceptions, and glib with verbalities and verbosities; and in the culture of these higher functions the peculiar sources of joy connected with our simpler functions often dry up, and we grow stone-blind and insensible to life's more elementary and general goods and joys.

The remedy under such conditions is to descend to a

* La Guerre et la Paix, Paris, 1884, vol. iii. pp. 268, 275, 316.

more profound and primitive level. To be imprisoned or shipwrecked or forced into the army would permanently show the good of life to many an over-educated pessimist. Living in the open air and on the ground, the lop-sided beam of the balance slowly rises to the level line; and the over-sensibilities and insensibilities even themselves out. The good of all the artificial schemes and fevers fades and pales; and that of seeing, smelling, tasting, sleeping, and daring and doing with one's body, grows and grows. The savages and children of nature, to whom we deem ourselves so much superior, certainly are alive where we are often dead, along these lines; and, could they write as glibly as we do, they would read us impressive lectures on our impatience for improvement and on our blindness to the fundamental static goods of life. "Ah! my brother," said a chieftain to his white guest, "thou wilt never know the happiness of both thinking of nothing and doing nothing. This, next to sleep, is the most enchanting of all things. Thus we were before our birth, and thus we shall be after death. Thy people, . . . when they have finished reaping one field, they begin to plough another; and, if the day were not enough, I have seen them plough by moonlight. What is their life to ours,—the life that is as naught to them? Blind that they are, they lose it all! But we live in the present."*

The intense interest that life can assume when brought down to the non-thinking level, the level of pure sensorial perception, has been beautifully described by a man who *can* write,—Mr. W. H. Hudson, in his volume, "Idle Days in Patagonia."

"I spent the greater part of one winter," says this admirable author, "at a point on the Rio Negro, seventy or eighty miles from the sea.

. . . "It was my custom to go out every morning on horseback with my gun, and, followed by one dog, to ride away from the valley; and no sooner would I climb the terrace, and plunge into the gray, universal thicket,

* Quoted by Lotze, Microcosmus, English translation, vol. ii. p. 240.

than I would find myself as completely alone as if five hundred instead of only five miles separated me from the valley and river. So wild and solitary and remote seemed that gray waste, stretching away into infinitude, a waste untrodden by man, and where the wild animals are so few that they have made no discoverable path in the wilderness of thorns. . . . Not once nor twice nor thrice, but day after day I returned to this solitude, going to it in the morning as if to attend a festival, and leaving it only when hunger and thirst and the westering sun compelled me. And yet I had no object in going,—no motive which could be put into words; for, although I carried a gun, there was nothing to shoot,—the shooting was all left behind in the valley. . . . Sometimes I would pass a whole day without seeing one mammal, and perhaps not more than a dozen birds of any size. The weather at that time was cheerless, generally with a gray film of cloud spread over the sky, and a bleak wind, often cold enough to make my bridle-hand quite numb. . . . At a slow pace, which would have seemed intolerable under other circumstances, I would ride about for hours together at a stretch. On arriving at a hill, I would slowly ride to its summit, and stand there to survey the prospect. On every side it stretched away in great undulations, wild and irregular. How gray it all was! Hardly less so near at hand than on the haze-wrapped horizon where the hills were dim and the outline obscured by distance. Descending from my outlook, I would take up my aimless wanderings again, and visit other elevations to gaze on the same landscape from another point; and so on for hours. And at noon I would dismount, and sit or lie on my folded poncho for an hour or longer. One day in these rambles I discovered a small grove composed of twenty or thirty trees, growing at a convenient distance apart, that had evidently been resorted to by a herd of deer or other wild animals. This grove was on a hill differing in shape from other hills in its neighborhood; and, after a time, I made a point of finding and using it as a resting-place every day at noon. I did not ask myself why I made choice of that one spot, sometimes going out of my way to sit there, instead of sitting down under any one of the millions of trees and bushes on any other hillside. I thought nothing about it, but acted unconsciously. Only afterward it seemed to me that, after having rested there once, each time I wished to rest again, the wish came associated with the image of that particular clump of trees, with polished stems and clean bed of sand beneath; and in a short time I formed a habit of returning, animal like, to repose at that same spot.

"It was, perhaps, a mistake to say that I would sit down and rest, since I was never tired; and yet, without being tired, that noon-day pause, during which I sat for an hour without moving, was strangely grateful. All day there would be no sound, not even the rustling of a leaf. One day, while *listening* to the silence, it occurred to my mind to wonder what the effect would be if I were to shout aloud. This seemed at the time a horrible suggestion, which almost made me shudder. But during those solitary days it was a rare thing for any thought to cross my mind. In the state of mind I was in, thought had become impossible. My state was one of *suspense* and *watchfulness*; yet I had no expectation of meeting an adventure, and felt as free from apprehension as I feel now while sitting in a room in London. The state seemed familiar rather than strange, and accompanied by a strong feeling of elation; and I did not know that something had come between me and my intellect until I returned to my former self,—to thinking, and the old insipid existence [again].

"I had undoubtedly *gone back*; and that state of intense watchfulness or alertness, rather, with suspension of the higher intellectual faculties, represented the mental state of the pure savage. He thinks little, reasons little, having a surer guide in his [mere sensory perceptions]. He is in perfect harmony with nature, and is nearly on a level, mentally, with the wild animals he preys on, and which in their turn sometimes prey on him."*

* *Op. cit.*, pp. 210-222 (abridged).

For the spectator, such hours as Mr. Hudson writes of form a mere tale of emptiness, in which nothing happens, nothing is gained, and there is nothing to describe. They are meaningless and vacant tracts of time. To him who feels their inner secret, they tingle with an importance that unutterably vouches for itself. I am sorry for the boy or girl, or man or woman, who has never been touched by the spell of this mysterious sensorial life, with its irrationality, if so you like to call it, but its vigilance and its supreme felicity. The holidays of life are its most vitally significant portions, because they are, or at least should be, covered with just this kind of magically irresponsible spell.

And now what is the result of all these considerations and quotations? It is negative in one sense, but positive in another. It absolutely forbids us to be forward in pronouncing on the meaninglessness of forms of existence other than our own; and it commands us to tolerate, respect, and indulge those whom we see harmlessly interested and happy in their own ways, however unintelligible these may be to us. Hands off: neither the whole of truth nor the whole of good is revealed to any single observer, although each observer gains a partial superiority of insight from the peculiar position in which he stands. Even prisons and sick-rooms have their special revelations. It is enough to ask of each of us that he should be faithful to his own opportunities and make the most of his own blessings, without presuming to regulate the rest of the vast field.

CHAPTER 3

What Makes a Life Significant

In MY previous talk, 'On a Certain Blindness,' I tried to make you feel how soaked and shot-through life is with values and meanings which we fail to realize because of our external and insensible point of view. The meanings are there for the others, but they are not there for us. There lies more than a mere interest of curious speculation in understanding this. It has the most tremendous practical importance. I wish that I could convince you of it as I feel it myself. It is the basis of all our tolerance, social, religious, and political. The forgetting of it lies at the root of every stupid and sanguinary mistake that rulers over subject-peoples make. The first thing to learn in intercourse with others is non-interference with their own peculiar ways of being happy, provided those ways do not assume to interfere by violence with ours. No one has insight into all the ideals. No one should presume to judge them off-hand. The pretension to dogmatize about them in each other is the root of most human injustices and cruelties, and the trait in human character most likely to make the angels weep.

Every Jack sees in his own particular Jill charms and perfections to the enchantment of which we stolid onlookers are stone-cold. And which has the superior view of the absolute truth, he or we? Which has the more vital insight into the nature of Jill's existence, as a fact? Is he in excess, being in this matter a maniac? or are we in defect, being victims of a pathological anæsthesia as regards Jill's magical importance? Surely the latter; surely to Jack are the profounder truths revealed; surely poor Jill's palpitating little life-throbs *are* among the wonders of creation, *are* worthy of this sympathetic interest; and it is to our shame that the rest of us cannot feel like Jack. For Jack realizes Jill concretely, and we do not. He struggles toward a union with her inner life, divining her feelings, anticipating her desires, understanding her limits as manfully as he can, and yet inadequately, too; for he is also afflicted with some blindness, even here. Whilst we, dead clods that we are, do not even seek after these things, but are contented that that portion of eternal fact named Jill should be for us as if it were not. Jill, who knows her inner life, knows that Jack's way of taking it— so importantly—is the true and serious way; and she responds to the truth in him by taking him truly and seriously, too. May the ancient blindness never wrap its clouds about either of them again! Where would any of *us* be, were there no one willing to know us as we really are or ready to repay us for *our* insight by making recognizant return? We ought, all of us, to realize each other in this intense, pathetic, and important way.

If you say that this is absurd, and that we cannot be in love with everyone at once, I merely point out to you that, as a matter of fact, certain persons do exist with an enormous capacity for friendship and for taking delight in other people's lives; and that such persons know more of truth than if their hearts were not so big. The vice of ordinary Jack and Jill affection is not its intensity, but its exclusions and its jealousies. Leave those out, and you see that the ideal I am holding up before you, however impracticable to-day, yet contains nothing intrinsically absurd.

We have unquestionably a great cloud-bank of ancestral blindness weighing down upon us, only transiently riven here and there by fitful revelations of the truth. It is vain to hope for this state of things to alter much. Our inner secrets must remain for the most part impenetrable by others, for beings as essentially practical as we are are necessarily short of sight. But, if we cannot gain much positive insight into one another, cannot we at least use our sense of our own blindness to make us more cautious in going over the dark places? Cannot we escape some of those hideous ancestral intolerances and cruelties, and positive reversals of the truth?

For the remainder of this hour I invite you to seek with me some principle to make our tolerance less chaotic. And, as I began my previous lecture by a personal reminiscence, I am going to ask your indulgence for a similar bit of egotism now.

A few summers ago I spent a happy week at the famous Assembly Grounds on the borders of Chautauqua Lake. The moment one treads that sacred enclosure, one feels one's self in an atmosphere of success. Sobriety and industry, intelligence and goodness, orderliness and ideality, prosperity and cheerfulness, pervade the air. It is a serious and studious picnic on a gigantic scale. Here you have a town of many thousands of inhabitants, beautifully laid out in the forest and drained, and equipped with means for satisfying all the necessary lower and most of the superfluous higher wants of man. You have a first-class college in full blast. You have magnificent music—a chorus of seven hundred voices, with possibly the most perfect open-air auditorium in the world. You have every sort of athletic exercise from sailing, rowing, swimming, bicycling, to the ball-field and the more artificial doings which the gymnasium affords. You have kindergartens and model secondary schools. You have general religious services and special club-houses for the several sects. You have perpetually running soda-water fountains, and daily popular lectures by distinguished men. You have the best of company, and yet no effort. You have no zymotic diseases, no poverty, no drunkenness, no crime, no police. You have culture, you have kindness, you have cheapness, you have equality, you have the best fruits of what mankind has fought and bled and striven for under the name of civilization for centuries. You have, in short, a foretaste of

what human society might be, were it all in the light,
with no suffering and no dark corners.

I went in curiosity for a day. I stayed for a week, held
spell-bound by the charm and ease of everything, by the
middle-class paradise, without a sin, without a victim,
without a blot, without a tear.

And yet what was my own astonishment, on emerging
into the dark and wicked world again, to catch myself
quite unexpectedly and involuntarily saying: "Ouf! what
a relief! Now for something primordial and savage, even
though it were as bad as an Armenian massacre, to set
the balance straight again. This order is too tame, this
culture too second-rate, this goodness too uninspiring.
This human drama without a villain or a pang; this community so refined that ice-cream soda-water is the utmost
offering it can make to the brute animal in man; this
city simmering in the tepid lakeside sun; this atrocious
harmlessness of all things,—I cannot abide with them.
Let me take my chances again in the big outside worldly
wilderness with all its sins and sufferings. There are the
heights and depths, the precipices and the steep ideals,
the gleams of the awful and the infinite; and there is
more hope and help a thousand times than in this dead
level and quintessence of every mediocrity."

Such was the sudden right-about-face performed for
me by my lawless fancy! There had been spread before
me the realization—on a small, sample scale of course—
of all the ideals for which our civilization has been striving: security, intelligence, humanity, and order; and here
was the instinctive hostile reaction, not of the natural
man, but of a so-called cultivated man upon such a
Utopia. There seemed thus to be a self-contradiction and
paradox somewhere, which I, as a professor drawing a full
salary, was in duty bound to unravel and explain, if I
could.

So I meditated. And, first of all, I asked myself what
the thing was that was so lacking in this Sabbatical city,
and the lack of which kept one forever falling short of

the higher sort of contentment. And I soon recognized that it was the element that gives to the wicked outer world all its moral style, expressiveness and picturesqueness,—the element of precipitousness, so to call it, of strength and strenuousness, intensity and danger. What excites and interests the looker-on at life, what the romances and the statues celebrate and the grim civic monuments remind us of, is the everlasting battle of the powers of light with those of darkness; with heroism, reduced to its bare chance, yet ever and anon snatching victory from the jaws of death. But in this unspeakable Chautauqua there was no potentiality of death in sight anywhere, and no point of the compass visible from which danger might possibly appear. The ideal was so completely victorious already that no sign of any previous battle remained, the place just resting on its oars. But what our human emotions seem to require is the sight of the struggle going on. The moment the fruits are being merely eaten, things become ignoble. Sweat and effort, human nature strained to its uttermost and on the rack, yet getting through alive, and then turning its back on its success to pursue another more rare and arduous still—this is the sort of thing the presence of which inspires us, and the reality of which it seems to be the function of all the higher forms of literature and fine art to bring home to us and suggest. At Chautauqua there were no racks, even in the place's historical museum; and no sweat, except possibly the gentle moisture on the brow of some lecturer, or on the sides of some player in the ball-field.

Such absence of human nature *in extremis* anywhere seemed, then, a sufficient explanation for Chautauqua's flatness and lack of zest.

But was not this a paradox well calculated to fill one with dismay? It looks indeed, thought I, as if the romantic idealists with their pessimism about our civilization were, after all, quite right. An irremediable flatness is coming over the world. Bourgeoisie and mediocrity, church sociables and teachers' conventions, are taking the place of the old heights and depths and romantic chiaroscuro. And, to get human life in its wild intensity, we must in future turn more and more away from the actual, and forget it, if we can, in the romancer's or the poet's pages. The whole world, delightful and sinful as it may still appear for a moment to one just escaped from the Chautauquan enclosure, is nevertheless obeying more and more just those ideals that are sure to make of it in the end a mere Chautauqua Assembly on an enormous scale. *Was im Gesang soll leben muss im Leben untergehn.* Even now, in our own country, correctness, fairness, and compromise for every small advantage are crowding out all other qualities. The higher heroisms and the old rare flavors are passing out of life.*

With these thoughts in my mind, I was speeding with the train toward Buffalo, when, near that city, the sight of a workman doing something on the dizzy edge of a sky-scaling iron construction brought me to my senses very suddenly. And now I perceived, by a flash of insight, that I had been steeping myself in pure ancestral blindness, and looking at life with the eyes of a remote spectator. Wishing for heroism and the spectacle of human nature on the rack, I had never noticed the great fields of heroism lying round about me, I had failed to see it present and alive. I could only think of it as dead and embalmed, labelled and costumed, as it is in the pages of romance. And yet there it was before me in the daily lives of the laboring classes. Not in clanging fights and desperate marches only is heroism to be looked for, but on every railway bridge and fire-proof building that is going up to-day. On freight-trains, on the decks of vessels, in cattleyards and mines, on lumber-rafts, among the firemen and the policemen, the demand for courage is incessant; and the supply never fails. There, every day of the year somewhere, is human nature *in extremis* for you. And wherever a scythe, an axe, a pick, or a shovel is

* This address was composed before the Cuban and Philippine wars. Such outbursts of the passion of mastery are, however, only episodes in a social process which in the long run seems everywhere tending toward the Chatauquan ideals.

wielded, you have it sweating and aching and with its powers of patient endurance racked to the utmost under the length of hours of the strain.

As I awoke to all this unidealized heroic life around me, the scales seemed to fall from my eyes; and a wave of sympathy greater than anything I had ever before felt with the common life of common men began to fill my soul. It began to seem as if virtue with horny hands and dirty skin were the only virtue genuine and vital enough to take account of. Every other virtue poses; none is absolutely unconscious and simple, and unexpectant of decoration or recognition, like this. These are our soldiers, thought I, these our sustainers, these the very parents of our life.

Many years ago, when in Vienna, I had had a similar feeling of awe and reverence in looking at the peasant-women, in from the country on their business at the market for the day. Old hags many of them were, dried and brown and wrinkled, kerchiefed and short-petticoated, with thick wool stockings on their bony shanks, stumping through the glittering thoroughfares, looking neither to the right nor the left, bent on duty, envying nothing, humble-hearted, remote;—and yet at bottom, when you came to think of it, bearing the whole fabric of the splendors and corruptions of that city on their laborious backs. For where would any of it have been without their unremitting, unrewarded labor in the fields? And so with us: not to our generals and poets, I thought, but to the Italian and Hungarian laborers in the Subway, rather, ought the monuments of gratitude and reverence of a city like Boston to be reared.

If any of you have been readers of Tolstoï, you will see that I passed into a vein of feeling similar to his, with its abhorrence of all that conventionally passes for distinguished, and its exclusive deification of the bravery, patience, kindliness, and dumbness of the unconscious natural man.

Where now is *our* Tolstoï, I said, to bring the truth

of all this home to our American bosoms, fill us with
a better insight, and wean us away from that spurious
literary romanticism on which our wretched culture—as
it calls itself—is fed? Divinity lies all about us, and culture
is too hide-bound to even suspect the fact. Could a
Howells or a Kipling be enlisted in this mission? or are
they still too deep in the ancestral blindness, and not
humane enough for the inner joy and meaning of the
laborer's existence to be really revealed? Must we wait for
some one born and bred and living as a laborer himself,
but who, by grace of Heaven, shall also find a literary
voice?

And there I rested on that day, with a sense of widening
of vision, and with what it is surely fair to call an increase
of religious insight into life. In God's eyes the differences
of social position, of intellect, of culture, of cleanliness,
of dress, which different men exhibit, and all the other
rarities and exceptions on which they so fantastically pin
their pride, must be so small as practically quite to vanish;
and all that should remain is the common fact that here
we are, a countless multitude of vessels of life, each of us
pent in to peculiar difficulties, with which we must
severally struggle by using whatever of fortitude and
goodness we can summon up. The exercise of the courage,
patience, and kindness, must be the significant portion of
the whole business; and the distinctions of position can
only be a manner of diversifying the phenomenal surface
upon which these underground virtues may manifest their
effects. At this rate, the deepest human life is everywhere,
is eternal. And, if any human attributes exist only in
particular individuals, they must belong to the mere
trapping and decoration of the surface-show.

Thus are men's lives levelled up as well as levelled
down,—levelled up in their common inner meaning,
levelled down in their outer gloriousness and show. Yet
always, we must confess, this levelling insight tends to
be obscured again; and always the ancestral blindness
returns and wraps us up, so that we end once more by
thinking that creation can be for no other purpose than to

develop remarkable situations and conventional distinctions and merits. And then always some new leveller in
the shape of a religious prophet has to arise—the Buddha,
the Christ, or some Saint Francis, some Rousseau or
Tolstoï—to redispel our blindness. Yet, little by little,
there comes some stable gain; for the world does get
more humane, and the religion of democracy tends toward permanent increase.

This, as I said, became for a time my conviction, and
gave me great content. I have put the matter into the
form of a personal reminiscence, so that I might lead you
into it more directly and completely, and so save time.
But now I am going to discuss the rest of it with you in a
more impersonal way.

Tolstoï's levelling philosophy began long before he
had the crisis of melancholy commemorated in that wonderful document of his entitled 'My Confession,' which
led the way to his more specifically religious works. In his
masterpiece 'War and Peace,'—assuredly the greatest of
human novels,—the rôle of the spiritual hero is given to
a poor little soldier named Karataïeff, so helpful, so cheerful, and so devout that, in spite of his ignorance and
filthiness, the sight of him opens the heavens, which
have been closed, to the mind of the principal character of
the book; and his example evidently is meant by Tolstoï
to let God into the world again for the reader. Poor little
Karataïeff is taken prisoner by the French; and, when too
exhausted by hardship and fever to march, is shot as
other prisoners were in the famous retreat from Moscow.
The last view one gets of him is his little figure leaning
against a white birch-tree, and uncomplainingly awaiting
the end.

"The more," writes Tolstoï in the work 'My Confession,' "the more I examined the life of these laboring
folks, the more persuaded I became that they veritably
have faith, and get from it alone the sense and the
possibility of life. . . . Contrariwise to those of our own
class, who protest against destiny and grow indignant
at its rigor, these people receive maladies and misfortunes

without revolt, without opposition, and with a firm and tranquil confidence that all had to be like that, could not be otherwise, and that it is all right so. . . . The more we live by our intellect, the less we understand the meaning of life. We see only a cruel jest in suffering and death, whereas these people live, suffer, and draw near to death with tranquillity, and oftener than not with joy. . . . There are enormous multitudes of them happy with the most perfect happiness, although deprived of what for us is the sole of good of life. Those who understand life's meaning, and know how to live and die thus, are to be counted not by twos, threes, tens, but by hundreds, thousands, millions. They labor quietly, endure privations and pains, live and die, and throughout everything see the good without seeing the vanity. I had to love these people. The more I entered into their life, the more I loved them; and the more it became possible for me to live, too. It came about not only that the life of our society, of the learned and of the rich, disgusted me—more than that, it lost all semblance of meaning in my eyes. All our actions, our deliberations, our sciences, our arts, all appeared to me with a new significance. I understood that these things might be charming pastimes, but that one need seek in them no depth, whereas the life of the hard-working populace, of that multitude of human beings who really contribute to existence, appeared to me in its true light. I understood that there veritably is life, that the meaning which life there receives is the truth; and I accepted it."*

In a similar way does Stevenson appeal to our piety toward the elemental virtue of mankind.

"What a wonderful thing," he writes,† "is this Man! How surprising are his attributes! Poor soul, here for so little, cast among so many hardships, savagely surrounded, savagely descended, irremediably condemned to prey upon his fellow-lives,—who should have blamed him, had he been of a piece with his destiny and a being merely bar-

* My Confession, X. (condensed).
† Across the Plains: "Pulvis et Umbra" (abridged).

barous? . . . [Yet] it matters not where we look, under
what climate we observe him, in what stage of society, in
what depth of ignorance, burdened with what erroneous
morality; in ships at sea, a man inured to hardship and
vile pleasures, his brightest hope a fiddle in a tavern, and
a bedizened trull who sells herself to rob him, and he, for
all that, simple, innocent, cheerful, kindly like a child,
constant to toil, brave to drown, for others; . . . in the
slums of cities, moving among indifferent millions to mechanical employments, without hope of change in the
future, with scarce a pleasure in the present, and yet true
to his virtues, honest up to his lights, kind to his neighbors, tempted perhaps in vain by the bright gin-palace,
. . . often repaying the world's scorn with service, often
standing firm upon a scruple; . . . everywhere some virtue cherished or affected, everywhere some decency of
thought and courage, everywhere the ensign of man's ineffectual goodness,—ah! if I could show you this! If I
could show you these men and women all the world
over, in every stage of history, under every abuse of
error, under every circumstance of failure, without hope,
without help, without thanks, still obscurely fighting the
lost fight of virtue, still clinging to some rag of honor,
the poor jewel of their souls."

All this is as true as it is splendid, and terribly do
we need our Tolstoïs and Stevensons to keep our sense
for it alive. Yet you remember the Irishman who, when
asked, "Is not one man as good as another?" replied,
"Yes; and a great deal better, too!" Similarly (it seems to
me) does Tolstoï overcorrect our social prejudices, when
he makes his love of the peasant so exclusive, and hardens
his heart toward the educated man as absolutely as he
does. Grant that at Chautauqua there was little moral
effort, little sweat or muscular strain in view. Still, deep
down in the souls of the participants we may be sure
that something of the sort was hid, some inner stress,
some vital virtue not found wanting when required. And,
after all, the question recurs, and forces itself upon us,
Is it so certain that the surroundings and circumstances

of the virtue do make so little difference in the importance of the result? Is the functional utility, the worth
to the universe of a certain definite amount of courage,
kindliness, and patience, no greater if the possessor of
these virtues is in an educated situation, working out far-
reaching tasks, than if he be an illiterate nobody, hewing
wood and drawing water, just to keep himself alive? Tolstoï's philosophy, deeply enlightening though it certainly
is, remains a false abstraction. It savors too much of that
Oriental pessimism and nihilism of his, which declares
the whole phenomenal world and its facts and their distinctions to be a cunning fraud.

A mere bare fraud is just what our Western common
sense will never believe the phenomenal world to be. It
admits fully that the inner joys and virtues are the *essential* part of life's business, but it is sure that *some* positive part is also played by the adjuncts of the show. If
it is idiotic in romanticism to recognize the heroic only
when it sees it labelled and dressed-up in books, it is
really just as idiotic to see it only in the dirty boots and
sweaty shirt of some one in the fields. It is with us really
under every disguise: at Chautauqua; here in your college;
in the stock-yards and on the freight-trains; and in the
czar of Russia's court. But, instinctively, we make a combination of two things in judging the total significance
of a human being. We feel it to be some sort of a product
(if such a product only could be calculated) of his inner
virtue *and* his outer place,—neither singly taken, but
both conjoined. If the outer differences had no meaning
for life, why indeed should all this immense variety of
them exist? They *must* be significant elements of the
world as well.

Just test Tolstoï's deification of the mere manual
laborer by the facts. This is what Mr. Walter Wyckoff,
after working as an unskilled laborer in the demolition of
some buildings at West Point, writes of the spiritual
condition of the class of men to which he temporarily
chose to belong:—

"The salient features of our condition are plain enough. We are grown men, and are without a trade. In the labor-market we stand ready to sell to the highest bidder our mere muscular strength for so many hours each day. We are thus in the lowest grade of labor. And, selling our muscular strength in the open market for what it will bring, we sell it under peculiar conditions. It is all the capital that we have. We have no reserve means of subsistence, and cannot, therefore, stand off for a 're- serve price.' We sell under the necessity of satisfying im- minent hunger. Broadly speaking, we must sell our labor or starve; and, as hunger is a matter of a few hours, and we have no other way of meeting this need, we must sell at once for what the market offers for our labor.

"Our employer is buying labor in a dear market, and he will certainly get from us as much work as he can at the price. The gang-boss is secured for this purpose, and thoroughly does he know his business. He has sole command of us. He never saw us before, and he will dis- charge us all when the débris is cleared away. In the mean time he must get from us, if he can, the utmost of physi- cal labor which we, individually and collectively, are capable of. If he should drive some of us to exhaustion, and we should not be able to continue at work, he would not be the loser; for the market would soon supply him with others to take our places.

"We are ignorant men, but so much we clearly see,— that we have sold our labor where we could sell it dearest, and our employer has bought it where he could buy it cheapest. He has paid high, and he must get all the labor that he can; and, by a strong instinct which possesses us, we shall part with as little as we can. From work like ours there seems to us to have been eliminated every element which constitutes the nobility of labor. We feel no personal pride in its progress, and no community of interest with our employer. There is none of the joy of responsibility, none of the sense of achievement, only the dull monotony of grinding toil, with the longing for the signal to quit work, and for our wages at the end.

"And being what we are, the dregs of the labor-market, and having no certainty of permanent employment, and no organization among ourselves, we must expect to work under the watchful eye of a gang-boss, and be driven, like the wage-slaves that we are, through our tasks.

"All this is to tell us, in effect, that our lives are hard, barren, hopeless lives."

And such hard, barren, hopeless lives, surely, are not lives in which one ought to be willing permanently to remain. And why is this so? Is it because they are so dirty? Well, Nansen grew a great deal dirtier on his polar expedition; and we think none the worse of his life for that. Is it the insensibility? Our soldiers have to grow vastly more insensible, and we extol them to the skies. Is it the poverty? Poverty has been reckoned the crowning beauty of many a heroic career. Is it the slavery to a task, the loss of finer pleasures? Such slavery and loss are of the very essence of the higher fortitude, and are always counted to its credit,—read the records of missionary devotion all over the world. It is not any one of these things, then, taken by itself,—no, nor all of them together,—that make such a life undesirable. A man might in truth live like an unskilled laborer, and do the work of one, and yet count as one of the noblest of God's creatures. Quite possibly there were some such persons in the gang that our author describes; but the current of their souls ran underground; and he was too steeped in the ancestral blindness to discern it.

If there *were* any such morally exceptional individuals, however, what made them different from the rest? It can only have been this,—that their souls worked and endured in obedience to some inner *ideal*, while their comrades were not actuated by anything worthy of that name. These ideals of other lives are among those secrets that we can almost never penetrate, although something about the man may often tell us when they are there. In Mr. Wyckoff's own case we know exactly what the self-imposed ideal was. Partly he had stumped himself, as the boys say, to carry through a strenuous achievement; but mainly he wished to enlarge his sympathetic insight into fellow-lives. For this his sweat and toil acquire a certain heroic significance, and make us accord to him exceptional esteem. But it is easy to imagine his fellows with various other ideals. To say nothing of wives and babies, one may have been a convert of the Salvation Army, and had a nightingale singing of expiation and forgiveness in his heart all the while he labored. Or there might have been an apostle like Tolstoï himself, or his compatriot Bondareff, in the gang, voluntarily embracing labor as their religious mission. Class-loyalty was undoubtedly an ideal with many. And who knows how much of that higher manliness of poverty, of which Phillips Brooks has spoken so penetratingly, was or was not present in that gang?

"A rugged, barren land," says Phillips Brooks, "is poverty to live in,—a land where I am thankful very often if I can get a berry or a root to eat. But living in it really, letting it bear witness to me of itself, not dishonoring it all the time by judging it after the standard of the other lands, gradually there come out its qualities. Behold! no land like this barren and naked land of poverty could show the moral geology of the world. See how the hard ribs . . . stand out strong and solid. No life like poverty could so get one to the heart of things and make men know their meaning, could so let us feel life and the world with all the soft cushions stripped off and thrown away. . . . Poverty makes men come very near each other, and recognize each other's human hearts; and poverty, highest and best of all, demands and cries out for faith in God. . . . I know how superficial and unfeeling, how like mere mockery, words in praise of poverty may seem. . . . But I am sure that the poor man's dignity and freedom, his self-respect and energy, depend upon his cordial knowledge that his poverty is a true region and kind of life, with its own chances of character, its own springs of happiness and revelations of God. Let him resist the characterlessness which often goes with being poor. Let him insist on respecting the condition where he lives. Let him learn to love it, so that by and by, [if] he grows rich, he shall go out of the low door of the old familiar poverty with a true pang of regret, and with a true honor for the narrow home in which he has lived so long."*

The barrenness and ignobleness of the more usual laborer's life consist in the fact that it is moved by no such ideal inner springs. The backache, the long hours, the danger, are patiently endured—for what? To gain a quid of tobacco, a glass of beer, a cup of coffee, a meal, and a bed, and to begin again the next day and shirk as much as one can. This really is why we raise no monument to the laborers in the Subway, even though they be our conscripts, and even though after a fashion our city is indeed based upon their patient hearts and enduring backs and shoulders. And this is why we do raise monuments to our soldiers, whose outward conditions were even brutaller still. The soldiers are supposed to have followed an ideal, and the laborers are supposed to have followed none.

You see, my friends, how the plot now thickens; and how strangely the complexities of this wonderful human nature of ours begin to develop under our hands. We have seen the blindness and deadness to each other which are our natural inheritance; and, in spite of them, we have been led to acknowledge an inner meaning which passeth show, and which may be present in the lives of others where we least descry it. And now we are led to say that such inner meaning can be *complete* and *valid for us also*, only when the inner joy, courage, and endurance are joined with an ideal.

But what, exactly, do we mean by an ideal? Can we give no definite account of such a word?

To a certain extent we can. An ideal, for instance, must be something intellectually conceived, something of which we are not unconscious, if we have it; and it must carry with it that sort of outlook, uplift, and bright-

* Sermons, 5th Series, New York, 1893, pp. 166, 167.

ness that go with all intellectual facts. Secondly, there
must be *novelty* in an ideal,—novelty at least for him
whom the ideal grasps. Sodden routine is incompatible
with ideality, although what is sodden routine for one
person may be ideal novelty for another. This shows that
there is nothing absolutely ideal: ideals are relative to the
lives that entertain them. To keep out of the gutter is
for us here no part of consciousness at all, yet for many
of our brethren it is the most legitimately engrossing of
ideals.

Now, taken nakedly, abstractly, and immediately, you
see that mere ideals are the cheapest things in life.
Everybody has them in some shape or other, personal or
general, sound or mistaken, low or high; and the most
worthless sentimentalists and dreamers, drunkards, shirks
and verse-makers, who never show a grain of effort,
courage, or endurance, possibly have them on the most
copious scale. Education, enlarging as it does our horizon
and perspective, is a means of multiplying our ideals, of
bringing new ones into view. And your college professor,
with a starched shirt and spectacles, would, if a stock of
ideals were all alone by itself enough to render a life
significant, be the most absolutely and deeply significant
of men. Tolstoï would be completely blind in despising
him for a prig, a pedant and a parody; and all our new
insight into the divinity of muscular labor would be altogether off the track of truth.

But such consequences as this, you instinctively feel,
are erroneous. The more ideals a man has, the more contemptible, on the whole, do you continue to deem him,
if the matter ends there for him, and if none of the
laboring man's virtues are called into action on his part,—
no courage shown, no privations undergone, no dirt or
scars contracted in the attempt to get them realized. It is
quite obvious that something more than the mere possession of ideals is required to make a life significant in
any sense that claims the spectator's admiration. Inner
joy, to be sure, it may *have*, with its ideals; but that is its
own private sentimental matter. To extort from us, out-

siders as we are, with our own ideals to look after, the
tribute of our grudging recognition, it must back its ideal
visions with what the laborers have, the sterner stuff of
manly virtue; it must multiply their sentimental surface
by the dimension of the active will, if we are to have
depth, if we are to have anything cubical and solid in the
way of character.

The significance of a human life for communicable
and publicly recognizable purposes is thus the offspring
of a marriage of two different parents, either of whom
alone is barren. The ideals taken by themselves give no
reality, the virtues by themselves no novelty. And let the
orientalists and pessimists say what they will, the thing of
deepest—or, at any rate, of comparatively deepest—significance in life does seem to be its character of *progress*,
or that strange union of reality with ideal novelty which
it continues from one moment to another to present. To
recognize ideal novelty is the task of what we call intelligence. Not every one's intelligence can tell which novelties are ideal. For many the ideal thing will always seem
to cling still to the older more familiar good. In this case
character, though not significant totally, may be still
significant pathetically. So, if we are to choose which is
the more essential factor of human character, the fighting
virtue or the intellectual breadth, we must side with
Tolstoï, and choose that simple faithfulness to his light
or darkness which any common unintellectual man can
show.

But, with all this beating and tacking on my part, I fear
you take me to be reaching a confused result. I seem to
be just taking things up and dropping them again. First
I took up Chautauqua, and dropped that; then Tolstoï
and the heroism of common toil, and dropped them;
finally, I took up ideals, and seem now almost dropping
those. But please observe in what sense it is that I drop
them. It is when they pretend *singly* to redeem life from
insignificance. Culture and refinement all alone are not
enough to do so. Ideal aspirations are not enough, when

uncombined with pluck and will. But neither are pluck and will, dogged endurance and insensibility to danger enough, when taken all alone. There must be some sort of fusion, some chemical combination among these principles, for a life objectively and thoroughly significant to result.

Of course, this is a somewhat vague conclusion. But in a question of significance, of worth, like this, conclusions can never be precise. The answer of appreciation, of sentiment, is always a more or a less, a balance struck by sympathy, insight, and good will. But it is an answer, all the same, a real conclusion. And, in the course of getting it, it seems to me that our eyes have been opened to many important things. Some of you are, perhaps, more livingly aware than you were an hour ago of the depths of worth that lie around you, hid in alien lives. And, when you ask how much sympathy you ought to bestow, although the amount is, truly enough, a matter of ideal on your own part, yet in this notion of the combination of ideals with active virtues you have a rough standard for shaping your decision. In any case, your imagination is extended. You divine in the world about you matter for a little more humility on your own part, and tolerance, reverence, and love for others; and you gain a certain inner joyfulness at the increased importance of our common life. Such joyfulness is a religious inspiration and an element of spiritual health, and worth more than large amounts of that sort of technical and accurate information which we professors are supposed to be able to impart.

To show the sort of thing I mean by these words, I will just make one brief practical illustration, and then close.

We are suffering to-day in America from what is called the labor-question; and, when you go out into the world, you will each and all of you be caught up in its perplexities. I use the brief term labor-question to cover all sorts of anarchistic discontents and socialistic projects, and the conservative resistances which they provoke. So far as this conflict is unhealthy and regrettable,—and I think it is so only to a limited extent,—the unhealthiness consists solely in the fact that one-half of our fellow-countrymen remain entirely blind to the internal significance of the lives of the other half. They miss the joys and sorrows, they fail to feel the moral virtue, and they do not guess the presence of the intellectual ideals. They are at cross-purposes all along the line, regarding each other as they might regard a set of dangerously gesticulating automata, or, if they seek to get at the inner motivation, making the most horrible mistakes. Often all that the poor man can think of in the rich man is a cowardly greediness for safety, luxury, and effeminacy, and a boundless affectation. What he is, is not a human being, but a pocket-book, a bank-account. And a similar greediness, turned by disappointment into envy, is all that many rich men can see in the state of mind of the dissatisfied poor. And, if the rich man begins to do the sentimental act over the poor man, what senseless blunders does he make, pitying him for just those very duties and those very immunities which, rightly taken, are the condition of his most abiding and characteristic joys! Each, in short, ignores the fact that happiness and unhappiness and significance are a vital mystery; each pins them absolutely on some ridiculous feature of the external situation; and everybody remains outside of everybody else's sight.

Society has, with all this, undoubtedly got to pass toward some newer and better equilibrium, and the distribution of wealth has doubtless slowly got to change: such changes have always happened, and will happen to the end of time. But if, after all that I have said, any of you expect that they will make any *genuine vital difference* on a large scale, to the lives of our descendants, you will have missed the significance of my entire lecture. The solid meaning of life is always the same eternal thing,— the marriage, namely, of some unhabitual ideal, however special, with some fidelity, courage, and endurance; with some man's or woman's pains.—And, whatever or wherever life may be, there will always be the chance for that marriage to take place.

Fitz-James Stephen wrote many years ago words to this effect more eloquent than any I can speak: "The 'Great Eastern,' or some of her successors," he said, "will perhaps defy the roll of the Atlantic, and cross the seas without allowing their passengers to feel that they have left the firm land. The voyage from the cradle to the grave may come to be performed with similar facility. Progress and science may perhaps enable untold millions to live and die without a care, without a pang, without an anxiety. They will have a pleasant passage and plenty of brilliant conversation. They will wonder that men ever believed at all in clanging fights and blazing towns and sinking ships and praying hands; and, when they come to the end of their course, they will go their way, and the place thereof will know them no more. But it seems unlikely that they will have such a knowledge of the great ocean on which they sail, with its storms and wrecks, its currents and icebergs, its huge waves and mighty winds, as those who battled with it for years together in the little craft, which, if they had few other merits, brought those who navigated them full into the presence of time and eternity, their maker and themselves, and forced them to have some definite view of their relations to them and to each other."*

In this solid and tridimensional sense, so to call it, those philosophers are right who contend that the world is a standing thing, with no progress, no real history. The changing conditions of history touch only the surface of the show. The altered equilibriums and redistributions only diversify our opportunities and open chances to us for new ideals. But, with each new ideal that comes into life, the chance for a life based on some old ideal will vanish; and he would needs be a presumptuous calculator who should with confidence say that the total sum of significances is positively and absolutely greater at any one epoch than at any other of the world.

* Essays by a Barrister, London, 1862, p. 318.

I am speaking broadly, I know, and omitting to consider certain qualifications in which I myself believe. But one can only make one point in one lecture, and I shall be well content if I have brought my point home to you this evening in even a slight degree. *There are compensations:* and no outward changes of condition in life can keep the nightingale of its eternal meaning from singing in all sorts of different men's hearts. That is the main fact to remember. If we could not only admit it with our lips, but really and truly believe it, how our convulsive insistencies, how our antipathies and dreads of each other, would soften down! If the poor and the rich could look at each other in this way, *sub specie æternatis,* how gentle would grow their disputes! what tolerance and good humor, what willingness to live and let live, would come into the world!